Spanish

HIPPOCRENE HANDY DICTIONARIES

For the traveler of independent spirit and curious mind, this practical series will help you to communicate, not just get by. Easier to use than a dictionary, the comprehensive listing of words and phrases is arranged alphabetically by key word. More versatile than a phrasebook, words frequently met in stores, on signs, or needed for standard replies, are conveniently presented by subject.

ARABIC
ISBN 0-87052-960-9

CHINESE
ISBN 0-87052-050-4

DUTCH
ISBN 0-87052-049-0

FRENCH
ISBN 0-7818-0010-2

GERMAN
ISBN 0-7818-0014-5

GREEK
ISBN 0-87052-961-7

ITALIAN
ISBN 0-7818-0011-0

JAPANESE
ISBN 0-87052-962-5

KOREAN
ISBN 0-7818-0082-X

PORTUGUESE
ISBN 0-87052-053-9

RUSSIAN
ISBN 0-7818-0013-7

SERBO-CROATIAN
ISBN 0-87052-051-2

SLOVAK
ISBN 0-7818-0101-1

SPANISH
ISBN 0-7818-0012-9

SWEDISH
ISBN 0-87052-054-7

THAI
ISBN 0-87052-963-3

TURKISH
ISBN 0-87052-982-X

Books may be ordered directly from the publisher. Each book costs $6.95. Send the total amount plus $3.50 for
Hippocrene Books, Inc.
171 Madison Avenue
New York, NY 10016.

HIPPOCRENE HANDY DICTIONARIES

Spanish

compiled by

LEXUS

with

Carmen Alonso-Bartol de Billinghurst,
Róger F Chaves Chavarría, Hugh O'Donnell
and Peter Terrell

HIPPOCRENE BOOKS
New York

11-9-93 6.26 B&T

Published in the United States of America in 1992 by
HIPPOCRENE BOOKS, INC., New York,
by arrangement with Routledge, London

For information, address:
HIPPOCRENE BOOKS, INC.
171 Madison Ave.
New York, NY 10016

ISBN 0-7818-0012-9

Contents

Spanish Pronunciation

Because you are likely to want to speak most of the Spanish given in this book, rather than just to understand its meaning, an indication of the pronunciation has been given in square brackets. If you pronounce this as though it were English, the result will be clearly comprehensible to a Spanish person.

In some cases, however, we have decided it was not necessary to give the entire pronunciation for a word or phrase. This may be because it would more or less duplicate the ordinary Spanish spelling, or because the pronunciation of a particular word or words has already been given within the same entry. In these cases we have simply shown how to pronounce the problematic parts of the word or phrase.

Some comments on the pronunciation system used:

VOWELS

a	as in 'path', 'garden'
ay	as in 'day'
o	as in 'ore'
oo	as in 'boot'

CONSONANTS

н	like the 'ch' sound in the Scottish pronunciation of 'loch'
r	always pronounced, never silent as in English

Where the print for a letter (or two letters) is in bold type this means that this part of the word should be stressed. It is very important to get the stress right when speaking Spanish.

English-Spanish

A

a un, una *[oon, oona]*; **90 pesetas a bottle** 90 pesetas la botella

about: about 25 unos 25; **about 6 o'clock** hacia las 6 *[ath-ya]*; **is the manager about?** ¿está el gerente por aquí? *[akee]*; **I was just about to leave** estaba a punto de salir *[... poonto ...]*; **how about a drink?** ¿quiere algo de beber? *[k-yairay]*

above por encima *[entheema]*; **above the village** encima del pueblo

abroad en el extranjero *[estrannay-ro]*

abscess un absceso *[apsthay-so]*

absolutely: it's absolutely perfect es maravilloso *[—beeyoso]*; **you're absolutely right** tiene toda la razón *[t-yenay]*; **absolutely!** ¡desde luego! *[dezday lway-go]*

absorbent cotton el algodón

accelerator el acelerador *[ath—]*

accept aceptar *[ath—]*

accident un accidente *[akthee—]*; **there's been an accident** ha habido un accidente *[... abeedo oon ...]*; **sorry, it was an accident** lo siento, ha sido sin querer *[kair-air]*

accommodation(s) alojamiento *[alonam-yento]*; **we need accommodation(s) for four** necesitamos habitación para cuatro *[... abeetath-yon ...]*

accurate exacto

ache: it aches me duele *[may dway-lay]*; **it aches here** me duele aquí *[akee]*

across: across the street al otro lado de la calle *[ka-yay]*

actor un actor

actress una actriz *[aktreeth]*

adapter un adaptador

address la dirección *[—kth-yon]*; **what's your address?** ¿cuál es su dirección? *[kwal]*

address book una libreta de direcciones *[deerekth-yonays]*

admission: how much is admission? ¿cuánto cuesta la entrada? *[kwanto kwesta]*

adore: I adore Spain me encanta España

adult un adulto *[adoolto]*

advance: I'll pay in advance pagaré por adelantado

advertisement un anuncio *[anoonth-yo]*

advise: what would you advise? ¿qué me aconseja? *[kay may akonsay-na]*

affluent rico

afraid: I'm afraid of heights me dan miedo las alturas *[... m-yaydo ...]*; **don't be afraid** no tengas miedo; **I'm not afraid** no tengo miedo; **I'm afraid I can't help you** me temo que no puedo ayudarle *[... taymo kay ...]*; **I'm afraid so** me temo que sí; **I'm afraid not** me temo que no

after: after you usted primero *[oostay preemairo]*; **after 9 o'clock** después de las 9 *[des-pways]*; **not until after 9 o'clock** no hasta después de las 9 *[no asta]*

afternoon la tarde *[tarday]*; **in the afternoon** por la tarde; **good afternoon** buenas tardes *[bwenas]*; **this afternoon** esta tarde

aftershave el 'aftershave'

after sun cream una crema para después del sol *[krayma ... despways ...]*

afterwards después *[despways]*

again otra vez *[beth]*

against contra

age edad *[ay-da]*; **under age** menor de edad; **not at my age!** ¡ya estoy demasiado viejo para eso! *[... daymas-yado b-yayno ...]*; **it takes ages** se tarda mucho; **I haven't been here for ages** hace años que no he estado aquí *[athay an-yos kay no ay estado akee]*

agency la agencia *[anenth-ya]*

ago: a year ago hace un año *[athay oon anyo]*; **it wasn't long ago** no hace mucho tiempo [t-yempo]

agony: it's agony es un dolor muy agudo [mwee agoodo]

aggressive agresivo [—eebo]

agree: do you agree? ¿estás de acuerdo? [day akwairdo]; **I agree** estoy de acuerdo; **fish doesn't agree with me** no me sienta bien el pescado

AIDS el SIDA [seeda]

air el aire [eye-ray]; **by air** en avión [ab-yon]

air-conditioning el aire acondicionado [eye-ray akondeeth-yonado]

air hostess la azafata [athafata]

airmail: by airmail por avión [ab-yon]

airmail envelope un sobre aéreo [sobray a-airayo]

airplane el avión [ab-yon]

airport el aeropuerto [a-airo-pwairto]

airport bus el autobús del aeropuerto [owtoboos]

airport tax el impuesto de aeropuerto [eempwesto]

alarm la alarma

alarm clock un despertador

alcohol el alcohol [alkol]

alcoholic: is it alcoholic? ¿tiene alcohol? [t-yenay]

Algeria Argelia [arHel-ya]

alive vivo [beebo]; **is he still alive?** ¿está vivo? [beebo]

all: all the hotels todos los hoteles; **all my money** todo mi dinero; **all of it** todo; **all of them** todos ellos [eyos]; **that's all** eso es todo; **all right** de acuerdo [day akwairdo]; **I'm all right** estoy bien [b-yen]; **all right!** ¡bien! [b-yen]; **it's all changed** ha cambiado todo; **thank you — not at all** gracias — de nada [day nada]

allergic: I'm allergic to ... soy alérgico a ... [alair-Heeko]

allergy una alergia [alair-Heea]

all-inclusive todo incluido [eenklweedo]

allowed permitido; **is it allowed?** ¿está permitido?; **I'm not allowed to eat salt** no puedo tomar sal [no pway-do]

almost casi

alone solo; **are you alone?** ¿está solo?; **leave me alone** déjeme en paz [day-Haymay em path]

already ya

also también [tamb-yen]

alteration (to plans) un cambio; (to clothes)

un arreglo

alternative: is there an alternative? (meal etc) ¿hay otra cosa? [eye]; **we had no alternative** no podíamos hacer otra cosa [... athair ...]

alternator un alternador

although aunque [a-oonkay]

altogether del todo; **what does that come to altogether?** ¿cuánto es todo? [kwanto]

always siempre [s-yempray]

a.m.: at 8 a.m. a las 8 de la mañana [day la man-yana]

amazing (surprising) increíble [eenkray-eeblay]; (very good) estupendo [estoo-pendo]

ambassador el embajador [emba-Hador]

ambulance una ambulancia [amboo-lanth-ya]; **get an ambulance!** ¡llame una ambulancia! [yamay]

America América

American americano/a

American plan la pensión completa [pens-yon]

among entre [entray]

amp: a 15-amp fuse un fusible de quince amperios [foo-see-blay]

an(a)esthetic la anestesia [anestays-ya]

ancestor un antepasado

anchor el ancla

anchovies unas anchoas

ancient antiguo [anteegwo]

and y [ee]

angina la angina [an-Heena]

angry enfadado; **I'm very angry about it** estoy muy enfadado por eso [... mwee ...]

animal un animal

ankle el tobillo [tobee-yo]

anniversary: it's our (wedding) **anniversary today** hoy es nuestro aniversario (de boda) [oy es nwestro aneebairsar-yo]

annoy: he's annoying me me está molestando [may]; **it's so annoying** es un fastidio

anorak un anorak

another: can we have another room? ¿puede darnos otra habitación? [pway-day]; **another bottle, please** otra botella, por favor

answer: there was no answer no hubo respuesta [no oobo respwesta]; **what was his answer?** ¿qué respondió? [kay respond-yo]

ant: ants las hormigas [ormeegas]

antibiotics unos antibióticos *[antee—]*

anticlimax una desilusión *[deseeloos-yon]*

antifreeze el anticongelante *[antee-kon-нelantay]*

antihistamine un antihistamínico *[antee-eestameeneeko]*

antique: is it an antique? ¿es antiguo? *[anteegwo]*; **antique shop** la tienda de antigüedades *[t-yenda day anteegway-dadays]*

antisocial: don't be antisocial no seas antipático *[no say-as]*

any: have you got any rolls/milk? ¿tiene bollos/leche? *[t-yenay]*; **I haven't got any** no tengo

anybody cualquiera *[kwalk-yay-ra]*; **can anybody help?** ¿alguien puede ayudar? *[alg-yen pway-day]*; **there wasn't anybody there** allí no había nadie *[no abee-a nad-yay]*

anything algo; **I don't want anything** no quiero nada *[no k-yairo nada]*; **don't you have anything else?** ¿no tiene nada más? *[… t-yenay …]*

apart from aparte de *[apartay day]*

apartment el apartamento

aperitif un aperitivo *[—eebo]*

apology una disculpa; **please accept my apologies** por favor, acepte mis disculpas *[… atheptay …]*

appalling terrible *[terreeblay]*

appear: it would appear that … parece que … *[parethay kay]*

appendicitis una apendicitis *[—thee-tees]*

appetite apetito; **I've lost my appetite** he perdido el apetito *[ay]*

apple una manzana *[manthana]*

apple pie una tarta de manzana

application form un impreso de solicitud *[eempreso day soleetheetood]*

appointment una cita *[theeta]*; **I'd like to make an appointment** (*with doctor*) quisiera pedir hora *[kees-yaira ped-eer ora]*

appreciate: thank you, I appreciate it se lo agradezco *[say lo agradethko]*

approve: she doesn't approve no le parece bien *[no lay parethay b-yen]*

apricot un albaricoque *[albareekokay]*

April abril

aqualung una botella de oxígeno *[bote-ya day oxee-нeno]*

Arab árabe *[ara-bay]*

archaeology la arqueología *[arkay-olo-нee-a]*

are *see pages 110, 115*

area: I don't know the area no conozco la zona *[thona]*

area code el prefijo *[prefee-нo]*

arena (*for bullfight*) el ruedo *[rway-do]*

arm el brazo *[bratho]*

around *see* **about**

arrangement: will you make the arrangements? ¿puede arreglarlo? *[pway-day]*

arrest (*verb*) detener; **he's been arrested** le han detenido *[lay an]*

arrival la llegada *[yegada]*

arrive: when do we arrive? ¿cuándo llegamos? *[kwando yegamos]*; **has my parcel arrived yet?** ¿ha llegado mi paquete? *[a yegado]*; **let me know as soon as they arrive** avíseme en cuanto lleguen *[abeesay-may en kwanto yegen]*; **we only arrived yesterday** llegamos sólo ayer

art el arte *[artay]*

art gallery el museo de bellas artes *[moo-sayo day beyas artes]*

arthritis una artritis *[—eetees]*

artificial artificial *[arteefeeth-yal]*

artist un pintor

as: as fast as you can tan rápido como puedas *[pway-das]*; **as much as you can** todo lo que pueda *[pway-da]*; **as you like** como usted quiera *[oostay k-yaira]*; **as it's getting late** ya que se está haciendo tarde *[… ath-yendo …]*

ashore: to go ashore desembarcar

ashtray un cenicero *[thenee-thairo]*

aside from aparte de *[apartay day]*

ask preguntar *[pregoontar]*; **that's not what I asked for** no es lo que he pedido *[kay ay pedeedo]*; **could you ask him to phone me back?** ¿puede decirle que me llame por teléfono? *[pway-day detheer-lay kay]*

asleep: he's still asleep todavía está durmiendo *[doorm-yendo]*

asparagus un espárrago

aspirin una aspirina

assault: she's been assaulted la han atacado *[la an]*; **indecent assault** un atentado contra el pudor *[poodor]*

assistant (*helper, in shop*) un empleado [*emplay-ado*]

assume: I assume that ... supongo que ... [*soopongo kay*]

asthma asma

astonishing increíble [*eenkray-eeblay*]

at: at the cafe en el café; **at the hotel** en el hotel; **at 8 o'clock** a las ocho; **see you at dinner** hasta la hora de cenar [*asta*]

Atlantic el Atlántico

atmosphere la atmósfera

attractive atractivo [*-eebo*]; **you're very attractive** eres muy atractiva [*... mwee ...*]

aubergine una berenjena [*beren-нay-na*]

auction una subasta [*soobasta*]

audience el público [*poo—*]

August agosto

aunt: my aunt mi tía

au pair (girl) la au-pair

Australia Australia [*owstral-ya*]

Australian australiano/a

Austria Austria [*owstr-ya*]

authorities las autoridades [*owtoreedades*]

automatic (*also car*) automático [*owto—*]

automobile el coche [*kochay*]

autumn el otoño [*oton-yo*]; **in the autumn** en otoño

available: when will it be available? ¿cuándo estará listo? [*kwando*]; **when will he be available?** ¿cuándo puedo verle? [*kwando pway-do bair-lay*]

avenue la avenida [*abeneeda*]

average: the average Spaniard el español medio [*mayd-yo*]; **an above average hotel** un hotel mejor de lo normal [*me-нor day lo normal*]; **a below average hotel** un hotel peor de lo normal [*... pay-or ...*]; **the food was only average** la comida era regular [*regoolar*]; **on average** por término medio

awake: is she awake yet? ¿está ya despierta? [*desp-yairta*]

away: is it far away? ¿está lejos? [*lay-нos*]; **go away!** ¡lárguese! [*largaysay*]

awful terrible [*teeree-blay*]

axle el eje [*e-нay*]

B

baby un bebé [*baybay*]

baby-carrier un capacho

baby-sitter una niñera [*neen-yaira*]; **can you get us a baby-sitter?** ¿podría conseguirnos a alguien que nos cuide al niño? [*podree-a konsegeeernos algyen kay nos kweeday al neenyo*]

bachelor soltero

back: I've got a bad back padezco de la columna [*padeth-ko*]; **at the back** en la parte de atrás; **in the back of the car** en la parte trasera del coche [*kochay*]; **I'll be right back** enseguida vuelvo [*ensegeeda bwelbo*]; **when do you want it back?** ¿cuándo quiere que se lo devuelva? [*kwando k-yairay kay say lo debwelba*]; **can I have my money back?** ¿puede devolverme el dinero? [*pway-day de-*]

bolbair-may]; **come back!** ¡vuelva! [*bwelba*]; **I go back home tomorrow** vuelvo a casa mañana [*bwelbo*]; **we'll go back next year** volveremos el año que viene [*bolbair-aymos el anyo kay b-yenay*]; **when is the last bus back?** ¿a qué hora es el último autobús? [*owtoboos*]; **he backed into me** retrocedió contra mí [*retrothed-yo ... mee*]

backache dolor de espalda; (*in kidneys*) dolor de riñones [*reen-yonays*]

back door la puerta trasera [*pwairta*]

backgammon las tablas reales [*ray-alays*]

backpack una mochila [*mocheela*]

back seat el asiento trasero [*as-yento*]

back street la callejuela [*kakay-нwayla*]

bacon el bacon; **bacon and eggs** huevos

con bacon [*waybos*]
bad (*quality*) malo; **this meat's bad** esta
carne está mala; **a bad headache** un
fuerte dolor de cabeza [*fwairtay ... ka-
betha*]; **it's not bad** no está mal; **too bad!**
¡mala suerte! [*swairtay*]
badly: he's been badly injured ha sido
herido gravemente [*grabaymentay*]
bag una bolsa; (*handbag*) un bolso; (*suitcase*)
una maleta [*malayta*]
baggage el equipaje [*ekeepa-нay*]
baggage allowance el equipaje permitido [*ekeepa-нay pairmeeteedo*]
baggage check (*at station*) la consigna de
equipaje [*konseegna day ekeepa-нay*]
bakery la panadería [*—ee-a*]
balcony el balcón; **a room with a
balcony** una habitación con balcón
[*abeetath-yon*]; **on the balcony** en el
balcón
bald calvo [*kalbo*]
ball una pelota
ballet el ballet
ball-point pen un bolígrafo
banana un plátano
band (*mus*) la orquesta [*orkesta*]
bandage (*noun*) una venda [*benda*]; **could
you change the bandage?** ¿podría
cambiar el vendaje? [*benda-нay*]
bandaid una tirita
bank (*money*) el banco; (*of river*) la orilla
(del río) [*oree-ya*]; **when are the banks
open?** ¿a qué hora abren los bancos? [*a
kay ora*]
bank account una cuenta bancaria
[*kwenta*]
bar el bar; **when does the bar open?** ¿a
qué hora abre el bar? [*a kay ora*]; **let's
meet in the bar** nos vemos en el bar [*nos
baymos*]; **a bar of chocolate** una barra
de chocolate [*chokolatay*]
barbecue una barbacoa
barber el barbero [*barbairo*]
bargain: it's a real bargain es una verda-
dera ganga [*... bairdadaira gang-ga*]
barmaid la camarera [*kamaraira*]
barman el barman
barrette una horquilla [*orkee-ya*]
bartender (*pub*) el barman
basic: (*essential*) esencial [*essenth-yal*]; **the
hotel is rather basic** el hotel es muy
modesto; **will you teach me some basic
phrases?** ¿me enseñaría algunas frases

útiles? [*may ensenyaree-a ... ooteelays*]
basket un cesto [*thesto*]
bath un baño [*banyo*]; **can I take a bath?**
¿puedo bañarme [*pway-do banyarmay*];
could you give me a bath towel? ¿me
podría dar una toalla de baño? [*may
podree-a dar oona to-aya day*]
bathing bañarse [*banyar-say*]
bathing costume el traje de baño
[*tra-нay day banyo*]
bathtub la bañera [*banyaira*]
bathrobe el albornoz [*—oth*]
bathroom el cuarto de baño [*kwarto day
banyo*]; **a room with a private bathroom** una habitación con baño privado
[*abeetath-yon con banyo preebado*]; **can
I use your bathroom?** ¿puedo ir al baño?
[*pwaydo eer*]
bath salts las sales de baño [*salays*]
battery la batería [*bateree-a*]; **the battery's flat** la batería está descargada
bay la bahía [*ba-ee-a*]
be ser [*sair*]; **be reasonable** sea razonable
[*say-a rathonablay*]; **don't be lazy** no sea
vago [*say-a bago*]; **where have you
been?** ¿dónde ha estado?; **I've never
been to ...** nunca he estado en ... *see* **I,
you, he** *etc and page 115*
beach la playa [*ply-a*]; **on the beach** en la
playa; **I'm going to the beach** voy a la
playa [*boy*]
beach ball una pelota de playa [*ply-a*]
beach mat una esterilla de playa [*esteree-
ya day ply-a*]
beach towel una toalla de playa [*to-aya
day ply-a*]
beach umbrella una sombrilla de playa
[*—eeya*]
beads (*necklace*) un collar [*ko-yar*]
beans judías [*нoodee-as*]; **French beans**
judías verdes [*bairdays*]; **dried beans**
judías blancas; **broad beans** habas
[*abas*]
beard la barba
beautiful bonito; (*person*) guapo [*gwapo*];
thank you, that's beautiful perfecto,
gracias [*pairfecto*]
beauty salon salón de belleza [*beyetha*]
because porque [*porkay*]; **because of the
weather** debido al tiempo [*t-yempo*]
bed una cama; **single bed** una cama individual [*eendeebeedwal*]; **double bed** una
cama de matrimonio; **you haven't made**

my bed no ha hecho la cama *[no a ay-cho]*; **I'm going to bed** me voy a acostar *[may boy]*; **he's still in bed** aún está acostado *[a-oon]*

bed and breakfast habitación y desayuno *[abeetath-yon ee desayoono]*

bed clothes la ropa de cama

bed linen las sábanas

bedroom un dormitorio

bee una abeja *[abay-нa]*

beef carne de vaca *[baca]*

beer la cerveza *[thairbay-tha]*; **two beers, please** dos cervezas, por favor

before antes *[antays]*; **before breakfast** antes de desayunar; **before I leave** antes de marcharme; **I haven't been here before** no he estado aquí antes *[no ay … akee]*

begin: what does it begin? ¿cuándo empieza? *[kwando emp-yaytha]*

beginner un principiante *[preentheep-yantay]*; **I'm just a beginner** soy un principiante

beginning: at the beginning al principio *[preentheep-yo]*

behaviour el comportamiento

behind detrás; **the driver behind me** el conductor detrás de mí

beige beige *[bays]*

Belgium Bélgica *[bel-нeeka]*

believe: I don't believe you no le creo *[no lay kray-o]*; **I believe you** le creo *[lay kray-o]*

bell (*door*) el timbre; (*church*) la campana

belly-flop un panzazo *[panthatho]*

belong: that belongs to me eso es mío; **who does this belong to?** ¿de quién es esto? *[day k-yen]*

belongings: all my belongings todas mis pertenencias *[—enth-yas]*

below abajo *[aba-нo]*; **below the knee** debajo de la rodilla *[deba-нo day la rodeeya]*

belt un cinturón *[theentooron]*

bend (*in road*) una curva *[koorba]*

berries las bayas *[ba-yas]*

berth un camarote *[—otay]*

beside: beside the church al lado de la iglesia *[eeglays-ya]*; **sit beside me** siéntese a mi lado *[s-yentay-say]*

besides: besides that aparte de eso

best el mejor *[meнor]*; **the best hotel in town** el mejor hotel de la ciudad *[th-*

yooda]; **that's the best meal I've ever had** es la mejor comida de mi vida *[beeda]*

bet: I bet you 500 pesetas le apuesto quinientas pesetas *[apwesto]*

better mejor *[meнor]*; **that's better** eso está mejor; **are you feeling better?** ¿se siente mejor? *[say s-yentay]*; **I'm feeling a lot better** me siento mucho mejor *[may s-yento]*; **I'd better be going now** mejor me voy *[boy]*

between entre

beyond más allá *[a-ya]*; **beyond the mountains** más allá de las montañas *[montan-yas]*

bicycle una bicicleta *[beetheeklay-ta]*; **can we rent bicycles here?** ¿se pueden alquilar bicicletas aquí? *[say pway-den alkeelar … akee]*

bidet el bidé *[beeday]*

big grande; **a big one** uno grande; **that's too big** eso es demasiado grande *[demas-yado]*; **it's not big enough** no es suficientemente grande *[… soofeeth-yentaymentay …]*

bigger más grande

bike una bicicleta *[beetheeklayta]*; (*motorbike*) una motocicleta *[mototheeklayta]*

bikini un bikini

bill la cuenta *[kwenta]*; **could I have the bill, please?** la cuenta, por favor

billfold la cartera *[kartaira]*

billiards el billar *[bee-yar]*

bingo el bingo *[beengo]*

bird un pájaro *[pa-нaro]*

bird (*tm*) un bolígrafo

birthday el cumpleaños *[koomplay-anyos]*; **it's my birthday** es mi cumpleaños; **when is your birthday?** ¿cuándo es su cumpleaños? *[kwando]*; **happy birthday!** ¡feliz cumpleaños! *[feleeth]*

biscuit una galleta *[ga-yayta]*

bit: just a little bit for me sólo un poquito para mí *[pokeeto]*; **a big bit** un pedazo grande *[pedatho]*; **a bit of that cake** un pedazo de esa tarta; **it's a bit too big for me** es un poco grande para mí; **it's a bit cold today** hoy hace algo de frío *[oy athay]*

bite (*by flea etc*) una picadura *[peekadoo-ra]*; **do you have something for bites?** ¿tiene algo para las picaduras? *[t-yenay]*;

I've been bitten (*by insect*) me ha picado un bicho [*may a peek***a***do oon beecho*]
bitter (*taste etc*) amargo
bitter lemon bitter lemon
black negro [*nay-gro*] *see* **coffee**
black and white (*photograph*) en blanco y negro
blackout: he's had a blackout ha sufrido un desmayo [*dezma-yo*]
bladder la vejiga [*be-нeega*]
blanket una manta; **I'd like another blanket** ¿quisiera otra manta, por favor? [*kees-ya***i***ra*]
blast ¡maldición! [*maldeeth-yon*]
blazer una chaqueta sport [*chak***ay***-ta*]
bleach (*for loo etc*) la lejía [*le-нee-a*]
bleed sangrar; **he's bleeding** está sangrando
bless you! ¡Jesús! [*нay-soos*]
blind ciego [*th-yaygo*]
blinds las persianas
blind spot un punto ciego [*poonto th-yaygo*]
blister una ampolla [*ampo-ya*]
blocked (*road, pipe*) obstruido [*opstrweedo*]
block of flats el edificio de apartamentos [*edeefeeth-yo*]
blond (*adjective*) rubio [*roob-yo*]
blonde (*noun*) una rubia [*roob-ya*]
blood sangre [*sangray*]; **his blood group is ...** su grupo sanguíneo es ... [*soo groopo sang-geenay-o*]; **I have high blood pressure** tengo la tensión alta [*... tensyon ...*]
bloody mary un vodka con zumo de tomate [*bodka kon thoomo day tomatay*]
blouse una blusa [*bloosa*]
blow-out un pinchazo [*peenchatho*]
blue azul [*athool*]
blusher el colorete
board: full board pensión completa [*pens-yon*]; **half-board** media pensión [*mayd-ya*]
boarding house una casa de huéspedes [*wespedays*], una pensión [*pens-yon*]
boarding pass tarjeta de embarque [*tar-нayta day embarkay*]
boat un barco
body el cuerpo [*kwairpo*]; (*dead*) un cadáver [*kadabair*]
boil (*on skin*) un furúnculo [*fooroonkoolo*]; (*water*) hervir [*airbeer*]

boiled egg un huevo pasado por agua [*waybo ... agwa*]
boiling hot hirviendo [*eerbyendo*]
bomb una bomba [*bom-ba*]
bone un hueso [*wayso*]
bonnet (*car*) el capó
book un libro; **I'd like to book a table for two** quisiera reservar una mesa para dos personas [*kees-yaira resairbar*]
bookshop, bookstore una librería
boot (*footwear*) una bota; (*of car*) el portaequipaje [*porta-ekeepaнay*]
booze la bebida [*bebeeda*]; **I had too much booze** bebí demasiado [*bebee demas-yado*]
border (*of country*) la frontera
bored: I'm bored estoy aburrido [*aboorreedo*]
boring aburrido [*aboorreedo*]
born: I was born in ... nací en [*nathee*]
borrow: may I borrow ...? ¿puede prestarme ...? [*pway-day*]
boss el jefe [*нefay*]
both los dos; **I'll take both of them** me llevo los dos [*may yaybo*]; **we'll both come** vendremos los dos [*bendray-mos*]
bother: sorry to bother you lamento tener que molestarle; **it's no bother** no es ninguna molestia [*molest-ya*]; **it's such a bother** es tan molesto
bottle una botella [*bote-ya*]; **a bottle of wine** una botella de vino [*beeno*]; **another bottle, please** otra botella, por favor
bottle-opener un abrebotellas [*abraybote-yas*]
bottom (*of person*) el trasero [*trasairo*]; **at the bottom of the hill** al pie de la colina [*p-yay*]
bottom gear la primera velocidad [*belotheeda*]
bouncer el gorila [*goreela*]
bowels el intestino
bowling (*ten pin*) los bolos
bowling green el campo de bolos
bowls (*game*) los bolos
box una caja [*ka-нa*]
box lunch una bolsa con la comida
box office la taquilla [*takee-ya*]
boy un chico [*cheeko*]
boyfriend: my boyfriend mi amigo
bra un sujetador [*soo-нetador*]
bracelet una pulsera [*poolsaira*]

brake el freno; **there's something wrong with the brakes** no están bien los frenos; **can you check the brakes?** ¿podría revisarme los frenos? *[podree-a rebeesarmay]*; **I had to brake suddenly** tuve que frenar bruscamente *[toobay]*

brake fluid el líquido para frenos *[leekeedo]*

brake lining la guarnición del freno *[gwarneeth-yon]*

brandy un coñac *[kon-yak]*

brave valiente *[bal-yentay]*

bread el pan; **could we have some bread and butter?** ¿podría traernos pan y mantequilla? *[podree-a tra-airnos ... mantekee-ya]*; **some more bread, please** más pan, por favor; **white bread** pan blanco; **brown bread** pan moreno; **wholemeal bread** pan integral; **rye bread** pan de centeno *[thentay-no]*

break romper *[rompair]*; **I think I've broken my ankle** creo que me he roto el tobillo *[kray-o kay may ay]*; **it keeps breaking** se rompe constantemente

breakdown una avería *[aberee-a]*; **I've had a breakdown** he tenido una avería; **nervous breakdown** una crisis nerviosa *[kreesees nairb-yosa]*

breakfast el desayuno *[dessa-yoono]*; **English/full breakfast** el desayuno inglés; **continental breakfast** el desayuno continental

break in: somebody's broken in alguien ha entrado a robar *[algyen]*

breast el pecho

breast-feed amamantar

breath el aliento *[al-yento]*; **out of breath** sin aliento

breathe respirar; **I can't breathe** no puedo respirar *[no pway-do]*

breathtaking *(view etc)* impresionante

breeze la brisa

breezy: it's breezy hace viento *[athay byento]*

bridal suite la suite nupcial *[noopth-yal]*

bride la novia *[nob-ya]*

bridegroom el novio *[nob-yo]*

bridge el puente *[pwentay]*; *(card game)* el bridge

brief breve *[brebay]*

briefcase el portafolios

bright *(light etc)* brillante *[breeyantay]*; **bright red** rojo vivo *[roнo beebo]*

brilliant *(idea, person)* brillante *[breeyantay]*

bring traer *[tra-air]*; **could you bring it to my hotel?** ¿podría traérmelo a mi hotel? *[podree-a tra-airmay-lo a mee o-tel]*; **I'll bring it back** se lo devolveré *[say lo daybolbair-ay]*; **can I bring a friend too?** ¿podría traer a un amigo también?

Britain Gran Bretaña *[bretan-ya]*

British británico

brochure un folleto *[foyayto]*; **do you have any brochures on ...?** ¿tiene algún folleto sobre ...? *[t-yenay algoon foyayto sobray]*

broke: I'm broke no tengo una perra

broken roto; **you've broken it** lo ha roto; **it's broken** está roto

broken nose la nariz rota *[nareeth]*

brooch un broche

brother: my brother mi hermano *[mee airmano]*

brother-in-law: my brother-in-law mi cuñado *[koonyado]*

brown marrón; *(sun-tanned)* moreno; **I don't go brown** nunca me pongo moreno

brown paper papel de estraza *[estratha]*

browse: may I just browse around? ¿puedo echar una ojeada? *[pway-do ... oнay-ada]*

bruise un cardenal

brunette una morena

brush un cepillo *[thepee-yo]*; *(artist's)* un pincel *[peenthel]*

Brussels sprouts coles de Bruselas

bubble bath gel de baño *[нel day banyo]*

bucket un cubo *[koobo]*

buffet un buffet; *(on a train)* vagón restaurante *[bagon restow-rantay]*

bug *(insect)* bicho; **she's caught a bug** ha cogido un virus *[ko-нeedo oon beeroos]*

building un edificio *[edeefeeth-yo]*

bulb una bombilla *[bombeeya]*; **we need a new bulb** necesitamos una bombilla nueva *[netheseetamos ... nwayba]*

bull el toro

bull fight una corrida de toros

bull fighter un torero *[torairo]*

bull ring la plaza de toros *[platha]*; *(actual arena)* el ruedo *[rwaydo]*

bump: I bumped my head me golpeé la cabeza *[may golpay-ay]*

bumper el parachoques *[—chokays]*

bumpy (*road*) llena de baches [*yayna day bachays*]

bunch of flowers un ramo de flores

bungalow un chalet

bunion un juanete [*Hwanay-tay*]

bunk una litera [*leetaira*]

bunk beds literas [*leetairas*]

buoy una boya

burglar un ladrón

burn: do you have an ointment for burns? ¿tiene alguna pomada para las quemaduras? [*kaymadooras*]

burnt: this meat is burnt esta carne está quemada [*kaymada*]; **my arms are so burnt** me he quemado mucho los brazos [*may ay kaymado … brathos*]

burst: a burst pipe una cañería rota

bus un autobús [*owtoboos*]; **is this the bus for …?** ¿es éste el autobús que va a …?; **when's the next bus?** ¿cuándo sale el próximo autobús? [*kwando*]

bus driver el conductor

business un negocio [*negoth-yo*]; **I'm here on business** estoy aquí de negocios [*… akee …*]

bus station la estación de autobuses [*estath-yon day owtoboosays*]

bus stop la parada del autobús [*owtoboos*]; **will you tell me which bus stop I get off at?** ¿podría indicarme en qué parada tengo que bajar? [*podree-a …*]

**baHar*]*

bust el pecho

bus tour una gira en autobús [*Heera en owtoboos*]

busy (*street, restaurant etc*) concurrido; **I'm busy this evening** esta noche estoy ocupado; **the line was busy** la línea estaba ocupada [*leenay-a*]

but pero [*pairo*]; **not … but …** no … sino …

butcher (*shop*) la carnicería [*karneetheree-a*]

butter la mantequilla [*mantekeeya*]

butterfly una mariposa

button un botón

buy: I'll buy it lo compro; **where can I buy …?** ¿dónde puedo comprar …? [*… pway-do*]

by: by train/car/plane en tren/coche/avión; **who's it written by?** ¿quién lo escribió? [*k-yen*]; **it's by Picasso** es de Picasso; **I came by myself** vine solo [*beenay*]; **a seat by the window** un asiento junto a la ventana [*as-yento Hoonto*]; **by the sea** a orillas del mar [*oreeyas*]; **can you do it by Wednesday?** ¿lo puede hacer para el miércoles? [*lo pway-day athair*]

bye-bye ¡adiós! [*ad-yos*]

bypass (*road*) la carretera de circunvalación [*theerkoombalath-yon*]

C

cab un taxi

cabaret un cabaret

cabbage un repollo [*repo-yo*]

cabin (*on ship*) un camarote [*—otay*]

cable (*elec*) un cable [*kablay*]

cablecar un teleférico

cafe una cafetería

caffeine la cafeína [*kafay-eena*]

cake un pastel; **a piece of cake** un pedazo de tarta [*pedatho*]

calculator una calculadora [*kalkooladora*]

calendar un calendario

call: what is this called? ¿cómo se llama esto? [*komo say yama esto*]; **call the police!** ¡llame a la policía! [*yamay a la poleethee-a*]; **call the manager!** ¡llame al gerente! [*yamay al Hairentay*]; **I'd like to make a call to England** quisiera llamar a Inglaterra por teléfono [*kees-yaira yamar …*]; **I'll call back later** (*come back*) volveré más tarde [*bolbair-ay*]; (*phone back*) volveré a llamar [*bolbair-ay a yamar*]; **I'm expecting a call from**

London estoy esperando una llamada de Londres [... *yamada* ...]; **would you give me a call at 7.30 tomorrow morning?** ¿puede llamarme mañana por la mañana a las siete y media? *[pway-day yamarmay]*; **it's been called off** se ha cancelado *[say a kanthelado]*

call box una cabina telefónica

calm tranquilo *[trankeelo]*; **calm down!** ¡tranquilícese! *[trankeeleethay-say]*

Calor gas (*tm*) una bombona de gas

calories las calorías

camera una máquina de fotos *[makeena]*

camp: is there somewhere we can camp? ¿hay algún sitio dónde podamos acampar? *[eye algoon seet-yo]*; **can we camp here?** ¿se puede acampar aquí? *[say pway-day ... akee]*

campbed una cama de campaña

camping el camping

campsite un camping

can (*of beer etc*) una lata

can: can I ...? ¿puedo ...? *[pway-do]*; **can I leave this here?** ¿puedo dejar esto aquí? *[pway-do de-нar]*; **can you ...?** (singular polite form) ¿puede ...? *[pway-day]*; **can you swim?** ¿sabe nadar? *[sabay]*; **can he ...?** ¿puede ...? *[pway-day]*; **can we ...?** ¿podemos ...? *[podaymos]*; **can they ...?** ¿pueden ...? *[pway-den]*; **I can't ...** no puedo ... *[no pway-do]*; **he can't ...** no puede ... *[no pway-day]*; **can I keep it?** ¿puedo guardármelo? *[pway-do gwardarmaylo]*; **if I can** si puedo; **that can't be right** eso no puede ser *[pway-day sair]*

Canada el Canadá

Canadian canadiense *[kanad-yensay]*

canal un canal

Canaries Canarias

cancel anular *[anoolar]*; **can I cancel my reservation?** ¿puedo anular la reserva? *[pway-do ... resairba]*; **can we cancel dinner for tonight?** ¿podríamos cancelar la cena esta noche? *[podree-amos kanth-elar la thayna]*; **I cancelled it** lo he anulado

cancellation una cancelación *[kanthelath-yon]*

candle una vela *[bay-la]*

candy caramelos; **a piece of candy** un caramelo

canoe una canoa

can-opener un abrelatas

cap (*yachting etc*) una gorra; (*of bottle*) un tapón; (*of radiator*) la tapa; **bathing cap** un gorro de baño *[ban-yo]*

capital city la capital

capital letters letras mayúsculas *[mayooskoolas]*

capsize: it capsized zozobró *[thothobro]*

captain el capitán

car un coche *[kochay]*

carafe una garrafa

carat: is it 14 carat gold? ¿es oro de catorce quilates? *[keelatays]*

caravan una caravana *[—bana]*

caravan site un camping

carbonated (*drink*) con gas

carburettor, carburetor el carburador *[karboorador]*

card: do you have a (business) card? ¿tiene tarjeta? *[t-yenay tar-нayta]*

cardboard box una caja de cartón *[ka-нa]*

cardigan una chaqueta *[chakay-ta]*

cards las cartas; **do you play cards?** juega usted a las cartas? *[нway-ga oostay]*

care: goodbye, take care adiós, cuídese *[kweeday-say]*; **will you take care of this bag for me?** ¿puede usted guardarme esta bolsa? *[pway-day oostay gwardar-may esta]*; **care of ...** (*address*) (*c/o*) casa de (*c/d*)

careful: be careful tenga cuidado *[kweedado]*

careless: that was careless of you eso ha sido imprudente; **careless driving** conducción temeraria *[kondookth-yon]*

car ferry un ferry

car hire un alquiler de coches *[alkeelair]*

car keys las llaves del coche *[yabays]*

carnation un clavel *[klabel]*

carnival un carnaval *[—bal]*

car park un aparcamiento *[aparkam-yento]*

carpet la alfombra

car rental un alquiler de coches *[alkeelair]*

carrier bag una bolsa de plástico

carrot una zanahoria *[thana-or-ya]*

carry llevar *[yebar]*; **could you carry this for me?** ¿podría usted llevarme esto? *[podree-a oostay yebar-may esto]*

carry-all un bolso de viaje *[b-yaнay]*

carry-cot un capazo *[kapa-tho]*

car-sick: I get car-sick me mareo en el coche *[may maray-o ...]*

carton (*of cigarettes*) un cartón; **a carton of milk** un cartón de leche

carving una talla *[ta-ya]*

carwash (*place*) un lavacoches *[labakochays]*

case (*suitcase*) la maleta; **in any case** de todas formas; **in that case** en ese caso; **it's a special case** es un caso especial *[espeth-yal]*; **in case he comes back** en caso de que vuelva *[bwelba]*; **I'll take two just in case** me llevo dos por si acaso *[may yaybo]*

cash dinero *[deenairo]*; **I don't have any cash** no tengo dinero; **I'll pay cash** pagaré al contado *[pagaray]*; **will you cash a cheque/check for me?** ¿podría hacerme efectivo un cheque? *[podree-a athair-may efekteebo]*

cashdesk la caja *[kaна]*

cash dispenser el cajero automático *[kaнairo owtomateeko]*

cash register la caja *[kaна]*

casino el casino

cassette una cassette

cassette player, cassette recorder un cassette

castanets unas castañuelas *[kastanywelas]*

castle el castillo *[kasteeyo]*

casual: casual clothes la ropa de sport

cat un gato

catamaran un catamarán

catastrophe una catástrofe

catch: where do we catch the bus? ¿dónde se coge el autobús? *[donday say ko-нay el ow-toboos]*; **he's caught some strange illness** ha cogido una enfermedad rara *[koн-eedo]*

catching: is it catching? ¿es contagioso? *[kontaн-yoso]*

cathedral la catedral

Catholic católico

cauliflower una coliflor

cause la causa *[kowsa]*

cave una cueva *[kwayba]*

caviar el caviar *[kab-yar]*

ceiling el techo

celebrations las celebraciones *[thelebrath-yonays]*

celery el apio *[apyo]*

cellophane celofán *[thelofan]*

cemetery el cementerio *[thementair-yo]*

center el centro *[thentro] see also* **centre**

centigrade centígrado *[thentee—] see page 119*

centimetre, centimeter un centímetro *[thentee—] see page 117*

central central *[thentral]*; **we'd prefer something more central** preferimos algo más céntrico *[thentreeko]*

central heating la calefacción central *[kalefakth-yon thentral]*

central station la estación central *[estath-yon thentral]*

centre el centro *[thentro]*; **how do we get to the centre?** ¿cómo se llega al centro? *[... say yay-ga ...]*; **in the centre (of town)** en el centro (de la ciudad) *[thyooda]*

century: in the 19th/20th century en el siglo diecinueve/veinte

ceramics la cerámica *[thairameeka]*

certain cierto *[th-yairto]*; **are you certain?** ¿está usted seguro? *[esta oostay segooro]*; **I'm absolutely certain** estoy segurísimo

certainly desde luego *[dezday lway-go]*; **certainly not** desde luego que no

certificate un certificado *[thairteefeekado]*; **birth certificate** la partida de nacimiento *[natheem-yento]*

chain una cadena

chair una silla *[see-ya]*

chairlift un telesilla *[teleseeya]*

chalet un chalet

chambermaid una camarera *[kamaraira]*

champagne el champán

chance: quite by chance por casualidad *[kas-waleeda]*; **no chance!** ¡ni hablar! *[nee ablar]*

change: could you change this into pesetas? ¿puede cambiarme esto en pesetas? *[pway-day kamb-yar-may ...]*; **I haven't any change** no tengo nada suelto *[swelto]*; **can you give me change for a 1,000 peseta note?** ¿puede cambiarme 1.000 pesetas? *[pway-day]*; **do we have to change (trains)?** ¿tenemos que cambiar de tren?; **for a change** para cambiar; **you haven't changed the sheets** no ha cambiado las sábanas; **the place has changed so much** el sitio ha cambiado tanto; **do you**

want to change places with me? ¿quiere cambiarse de sitio conmigo? *[k-yairay kamb-yarsay]*; **can I change this for ...?** ¿puedo cambiar esto por ...? *[pway-do]*

changeable (*person*) inconstante; (*weather*) variable *[bar-yablay]*

channel: the English Channel el canal de la Mancha

chaos el desorden

chap un tipo; **the chap at reception** el señor de la recepción *[rethepth-yon]*

chapel una capilla *[kapeeya]*

charge: is there an extra charge? ¿hay suplemento? *[eye sooplay-mento]*; **what do you charge?** ¿cuánto cobra?; **who's in charge here?** ¿quién es el encargado aquí? *[k-yen]*

charming (*person*) encantador

chart (*sea*) la carta de navegación *[nabay-gath-yon]*

charter flight un vuelo chárter *[bwaylo]*

chassis el chasis

cheap barato; **do you have something cheaper?** tiene algo más barato? *[t-yenay]*

cheat: I've been cheated me han engañado *[may an engan-yado]*

check: will you check? ¿quiere asegurarse? *[k-yairay asegoorar-say]*; **will you check the steering?** ¿puede revisar la dirección? *[pway-day rebeesar]*; **will you check the bill?** ¿puede comprobar la factura? *[pway-day]*; **we checked in** nos inscribimos; **we checked out** dejamos el hotel *[deнamos]*; **I've checked it** lo he comprobado

check (*money*) un cheque *[chek-ay]*; **will you take a check?** ¿aceptan cheques? *[atheptan]*

check (*bill*) la cuenta *[kwenta]*; **may I have the check please?** la cuenta, por favor *[kwenta]*

checkbook un talonario de cheques *[che-kays]*

checked (*shirt etc*) de cuadros *[kwadros]*

checkers juego de damas *[нwaygo]*

check-in (*at airport*) el mostrador

checkroom el guardarropa *[gwarda-rropa]*

cheek la mejilla *[menee-ya]*; **what a cheek!** ¡qué cara!

cheeky descarado

cheerio hasta luego *[asta lway-go]*

cheers (*thank you*) gracias; (*toast*) salud *[saloo]*

cheer up! ¡anímate! *[aneematay]*

cheese el queso *[kay-so]*

cheesecake una tarta de queso *[kay-so]*

chef el cocinero *[kotheenairo]*

chemist una farmacia *[farmath-ya]*

cheque un cheque *[chek-ay]*; **will you take a cheque?** ¿aceptan cheques? *[atheptan]*

cheque book un talonario de cheques *[chek-ays]*

cheque card la tarjeta de banco *[tar-нayta]*

cherry una cereza *[thairaytha]*

chess el ajedrez *[aнedreth]*

chest el pecho

chewing gum un chicle *[cheek-lay]*

chicken el pollo *[po-yo]*

chickenpox la varicela *[bareethela]*

child un niño *[neenyo]*; **children** los niños

child minder una persona que cuida a los niños *[... kweeda ...]*

child minding service servicio para cuidar a los niños *[sairbeeth-yo para kweedar]*

children's playground un parque infantil *[parkay]*

children's pool una piscina infantil *[peestheena]*

children's portion una ración pequeña (para niños) *[rath-yon paykayn-ya]*

children's room la habitación de los niños *[abeetath-yon]*

chilled (*wine*) frío; **it's not properly chilled** no está suficientemente frío *[soofeeth-yentaymentay free-o]*

chilly (*weather*) frío

chimney una chimenea *[cheemenay-a]*

chin la barbilla *[barbee-ya]*

china la porcelana *[porthelana]*

chips unas patatas fritas

chiropodist un callista *[ka-yeesta]*

chocolate el chocolate *[—latay]*; **a chocolate bar** una barra de chocolate; **a box of chocolates** una caja de bombones *[ka-нa]*; **hot chocolate** una taza de chocolate *[tatha]*

choke (*car*) el aire *[eye-ray]*

choose: it's hard to choose es difícil elegir *[es deefeetheel ele-нeer]*; **you choose for us** elija usted *[elee-на* oostay]

chop: pork/lamb chop una chuleta de cerdo/de cordero [choolayta day thairdo/kordairo]

Christian name el nombre de pila

Christmas Navidad [nabeeda]; **merry Christmas** Feliz Navidad [feleeth]

church una iglesia [eeglays-ya]; **where is the Protestant/Catholic Church?** ¿dónde está la iglesia protestante/católica?

cider una sidra [seedra]

cigar un puro [pooro]

cigarette un cigarrillo [theegaree-yo]; **tipped/plain cigarettes** cigarrillos con filtro/sin filtro

cigarette lighter un encendedor [enthendedor]

cine-camera un tomavistas [tomabeestas]

cinema el cine [theenay]

circle un círculo [theerkoolo]; (theatre: seats) el anfiteatro

citizen: I'm a British/American citizen soy británico/a/americano/a

city una ciudad [th-yooda]

city centre, city center el centro de la ciudad [thentro day la th-yooda]

claim (insurance) una reclamación [reklamath-yon]

claim form (insurance) un impreso de reclamación (del seguro) [reklamath-yon]

clarify aclarar

classical clásico

clean limpio [leemp-yo]; **may I have some clean sheets?** ¿puede darme sábanas limpias? [pway-day darmay]; **our apartment hasn't been cleaned today** hoy no han limpiado el apartamento; **it's not clean** no está limpio; **can you clean this for me?** (clothes) ¿puede limpiarme esto? [pway-day leemp-yarmay]

cleansing cream una crema limpiadora

clear: it's not very clear (meaning) no está muy claro; **OK, that's clear** (understood) entendido

clever listo

cliff un acantilado

climate el clima

climb: it's a long climb to the top es una subida larga hasta la cima [asta la theema]

clinic una clínica

cloakroom (for coats) el guardarropa [gwardarropa]; **(WC)** los aseos [assayos]

clock el reloj [reloH]

close: is it close? ¿está cerca? [thairka]; **close to the hotel** cerca del hotel; **close by** muy cerca [mwee]; (weather) bochornoso

close: when do you close? ¿a qué hora cierra? [a kay ora th-yairra]

closed cerrado [thairrado]; **they were closed** estaba cerrado

closet un armario

cloth (material) una tela; (rag etc) un trapo

clothes la ropa

clothes line la cuerda para tender la ropa [kwairda]

clothes peg, clothespin una pinza de la ropa [peentha]

cloud una nube [noobay]; **it's clouding over** se está nublando

cloudy nublado [nooblado]

club un club [kloob]

clubhouse el chalet (del club)

clumsy patoso

clutch (car) el embrague [embragay]; **the clutch is slipping** patina el embrague

coach un autocar [owtokar]

coach party un grupo en autocar [owtokar]

coach trip una excursión (en autobús) [eskoors-yon]

coast la costa; **at the coast** en la costa

coastguard un guardacostas [gwardakostas]

coat (overcoat etc) un abrigo; (jacket) una chaqueta [chakay-ta]

coathanger una percha [paircha]

cobbled street una calle empedrada [kayay]

cobbler un zapatero [thapatairo]

cockroach una cucaracha [kookaracha]

cocktail un cóctel

cocktail bar el bar

cocoa (drink) cacao

coconut un coco

code: what's the (dialling) code for ...? ¿cuál es el prefijo para ...? [es el prefeeHo]

coffee un café [kafay]; **white coffee** un café con leche; **black coffee** un café solo; **two coffees, please** dos cafés, por favor; **brown coffee** un cortado (this is a very

small cup)
coin una moneda
Coke (*tm*) una Coca-Cola
cold frío; **I'm cold** tengo frío; **I have a cold** tengo catarro
coldbox (*for food*) una nevera *[naybaira]*
cold cream una crema limpiadora *[leemp-yadora]*
collapse: he's collapsed se ha desmayado *[say a desma-yado]*
collar el cuello *[kwe-yo]*
collar bone la clavícula *[klabeekoola]*
colleague: my colleague mi colega; **your colleague** su colega
collect: I've come to collect ... he venido a recoger ... *[ay beneedo a reko-наir]*; **I collect ...** (*stamps etc*) colecciono *[kolekth-yono]*; **I want to call New York collect** quiero llamar a Nueva York a cobro revertido *[k-yairo yamar ... rebairteedo]*
collect call una conferencia a cobro revertido *[konferenth-ya ... rebairteedo]*
college una escuela universitaria *[eskwayla ooneebairseetar-ya]*
collision un choque *[chokay]*
cologne una colonia
colo(u)r color; **do you have any other colo(u)rs?** ¿tiene otros colores? *[t-yenay]*
colo(u)r film una película en color
comb un peine *[pay-eenay]*
come venir *[beneer]*; **I come from London** soy de Londres; **where do you come from?** ¿de dónde eres?; **when are they coming?** ¿cuándo vienen? *[kwando b-yenen]*; **come here** venga aquí *[benga akee]*; **come with me** venga conmigo; **come back!** ¡vuelva! *[bwelba]*; **I'll come back later** volveré más tarde *[bolbair-ay]*; **come in!** ¡adelante!; **it just came off** se rompió *[romp-yo]*; **he's coming on very well** (*improving*) está mejorando *[meнorando]*; **it's coming on nicely** va muy bien *[ba mwee b-yen]*; **come on!** ¡vamos! *[bamos]*; **do you want to come out this evening?** ¿quieres salir esta noche? *[k-yairays]*; **these two pictures didn't come out** estas dos fotos no han salido; **the money hasn't come through yet** el dinero no ha llegado todavía *[yegado todabee-a]*
comfortable cómodo; **it's not very comfortable** no es muy cómodo *[...*

mwee ...]
Common Market el Mercado Común *[mair-kado komoon]*
company (*firm*) una compañía *[kompanyee-a]*
comparison: there's no comparison no se puede comparar *[... pway-day ...]*
compartment (*train*) un compartimento
compass una brújula *[broo-ноola]*
compensation una indemnización *[—thath-yon]*
complain quejarse *[akeнar-say]*; **I want to complain about my room** no estoy contento con mi habitación *[abeetath-yon]*
complaint una queja *[kay-нa]*
complete: the complete set un juego completo *[нway-go]*; **it's a complete disaster** es un desastre total
completely completamente
complicated: it's very complicated es muy complicado *[... mwee ...]*
compliment: my compliments to the chef felicite al cocinero de mi parte *[feleetheetay al kotheenairo]*
comprehensive (*insurance*) (un seguro) contra todo riesgo *[r-yesgo]*
compulsory obligatorio
computer una computadora
concern: we are very concerned estamos muy preocupados *[... mwee ...]*
concert un concierto *[konth-yairto]*
concussion una conmoción cerebral *[konmoth-yon therebral]*
condenser (*car*) el condensador
condition la condición *[kondeeth-yon]*; **it's not in very good condition** no está en muy buenas condiciones *[mwee bwenas kondeeth-yonays]*
conditioner (*for hair*) un acondicionador de pelo *[akondeeth-yonador]*
condom un condón
conductor (*rail*) el revisor *[rebeesor]*
conference un congreso
confirm: can you confirm that? ¿puede confirmarlo? *[pway-day]*
confuse: it's very confusing es muy complicado
congratulations! ¡enhorabuena! *[enorabwena]*
conjunctivitis conjunctivitis *[kon-ноonteebeetees]*
connection (*travel*) el enlace *[enlathay]*

connecting flight un vuelo de conexión *[bway-lo day koneks-yon]*

connoisseur un experto *[espairto]*

conscious consciente *[konsth-yentay]*

consciousness: he's lost consciousness ha perdido el conocimiento *[a pairdeedo el konotheem-yento]*

constipation estreñimiento *[estren-yeem-yento]*

consul el cónsul *[konsool]*

consulate el consulado

contact: how can I contact ...? ¿cómo puedo ponerme en contacto con ...? *[... pway-do pon-airmay ...]*; **I'm trying to contact ...** estoy intentando ponerme en contacto con ...

contact lenses unas lentillas *[lentee-yas]*

contraceptive un anticonceptivo *[antee-konthepteebo]*

continent: on the continent en el continente

convenient conveniente *[komben-yentay]*

cook: it's not properly cooked no está bien hecho *[b-yen aycho]*; **it's beautifully cooked** está muy rico; **he's a good cook** cocina muy bien *[kotheena mwee b-yen]*

cooker una cocina *[kotheena]*

cookie una galleta *[ga-yayta]*

cool fresco

corduroy la pana

cork el corcho

corkscrew un sacacorchos

corn *(foot)* un callo *[ka-yo]*

corner: on the corner en la esquina *[eskeena]*; **in the corner** en el rincón; **a corner table** una mesa tranquila *[trankeela]*

cornflakes los cornflakes

coronary un infarto

correct correcto; **please correct me if I make a mistake** por favor, corríjame si digo algo mal *[... korree-намay ...]*

corridor un pasillo *[paseeyo]*

corset una faja *[fa-на]*

cosmetics los cosméticos

cost: what does it cost? ¿cuánto cuesta? *[kwanto kwesta]*

cot una cuna

cotton el algodón

cotton buds bolas de algodón

cotton wool el algodón

couch un sofá

couchette una litera *[leetaira]*

cough la tos

cough drops unas pastillas para la tos *[pasteeyas]*

cough medicine una medicina para la tos *[medeetheena]*

could: could you ...? ¿podría ...? *[podree-a]*; **could I have ...?** quiero ... *[k-yairo]*; **I couldn't ...** no podría ...

country un país *[pa-ees]*; **in the country** en el campo

countryside el campo

couple *(man and woman)* una pareja *[paray-на]*; **a couple of ...** un par de ...

courier el guía turístico *[g-ee-a]*

course *(of meal)* un plato; **of course** por supuesto *[soopwesto]*

court *(law)* un tribunal *[treeboonal]* *(tennis)* una pista

courtesy bus el autobús privado *[owto-boos preebado]*

cousin: my cousin mi primo

cover charge la consumición mínima *[konsoomeeth-yon]*

cow una vaca *[baka]*

crab un cangrejo *[kangray-но]*

cracked: it's cracked está agrietado *[agr-yaytado]*

cracker un crácker

craftshop una tienda de artesanía *[t-yenda day artesanee-a]*

cramp *(in leg etc)* un calambre

crankshaft el eje del cigüeñal *[e-hay del theegway-nyal]*

crash: there's been a crash ha habido un accidente *[a abeedo oon aktheedentay]*

crash course un curso intensivo *[koorso eentenseebo]*

crash helmet un casco

crawl *(swimming)* el crol

crazy loco

cream *(on milk, on cakes)* la nata; *(for skin)* la crema; *(colour)* color crema

cream cheese un queso de nata *[kayso]*

creche una guardería infantil *[gwardair-ee-a]*

credit card una tarjeta de crédito *[tar-найta]*

crib *(for baby)* una cuna *[koona]*

crisis la crisis *[kreeses]*

crisps unas patatas fritas (a la inglesa)

crockery la loza *[lotha]*

crook: he's a crook es un estafador
crossing (*by boat*) la travesía
[*trabesee-a*]
crossroads un cruce [*kroothay*]
crosswalk un paso de peatones [*pay-atonays*]
crowd la muchedumbre [*moochay-doombray*]
crowded lleno [*yayno*]
crown (*on tooth*) una funda [*foonda*]
crucial: it's absolutely crucial es muy importante [*... mwee ...*]
cruise un crucero [*kroothairo*]
crutch una muleta [*moolay-ta*]; (*of body*) las ingles [*eenglays*]
cry llorar [*yorar*]; **don't cry** no llore [*no yoray*]
cucumber un pepino
cuisine la cocina [*kotheena*]
cultural cultural [*kooltooral*]
cup una taza [*tatha*]; **a cup of coffee** un café [*kafay*]
cupboard un armario [*armar-yo*]
cure: can you cure it? ¿puede curarlo? [*pway-day*]

curlers los rulos [*roolos*]
current la corriente [*korr-yentay*]
curry 'curry' [*kooree*]
curtains las cortinas
curve una curva [*koorba*]
cushion un cojín [*ko-неen*]
custom la costumbre [*kostoombray*]
Customs la aduana [*adwana*]
cut: I've cut myself me he cortado; **could you cut a little off here?** ¿puede cortar un poco de aquí? [*pway-day... akee*]; **we were cut off** nos han cortado; **the engine keeps cutting out** el motor se cala mucho
cutlery cubiertos [*koob-yairtos*]
cutlet una chuleta [*choolay-ta*]
cycle: can we cycle there? ¿se puede ir en bicicleta? [*pway-day eer em beetheeklay-ta*]
cyclist un ciclista [*theekleesta*]
cylinder un cilindro [*theeleendro*]
cylinder-head gasket la junta de culata [*ноonta*]
cynical cínico [*theeneeko*]
cystitis una cistitis [*theesteetees*]

D

damage: you've damaged it lo ha estropeado [*estropay-ado*]; **it's damaged** es defectuoso [*defekt-woso*]; **there's no damage** no está estropeado [*estropay-ado*]
damn! ¡maldita sea! [*say-a*]
damp húmedo [*oomaydo*]
dance: a Spanish dance un baile español [*by-lay*]; **do you want to dance?** ¿quiere bailar? [*k-yairay by-lar*]
dancer: he's a good dancer baila muy bien [*by-la mwee b-yen*]
dancing: we'd like to go dancing nos gustaría ir a bailar [*by-lar*]; **traditional Spanish dancing** un baile popular español [*by-lay popoolar*]
dandruff la caspa
dangerous peligroso

dare: I don't dare no me atrevo [*atraybo*]
dark oscuro [*oskooro*]; **dark blue** azul oscuro [*athool*]; **when does it get dark?** ¿a qué hora oscurece? [*a kay ora oskoorethay*]; **after dark** después de anochecer [*anochay-thair*]
darling querido [*kaireedo*]; (*to woman*) querida [*kaireeda*]
darts los dardos
dashboard el tablero de instrumentos
date: what's the date? ¿qué día es hoy? [*kay dee-a es oy*]; **on what date?** ¿en qué fecha?; **can we make a date?** ¿podemos citarnos? [*theetarnos*]
dates (*to eat*) unos dátiles [*dateelays*]
daughter: my daughter mi hija [*mee ee-на*]
daughter-in-law la nuera [*nwaira*]

dawn el amanecer *[amanethair]*; **at dawn** al amanecer

day el día *[dee-a]*; **the day after** el día siguiente *[seeg-yentay]*; **the day before** el día antes; **every day** todos los días; **one day** un día; **can we pay by the day?** ¿podemos pagar cada día?; **have a good day!** ¡qué pase un buen día! *[bwen dee-a]*

daylight robbery un robo

day trip una excursión *[eskoors-yon]*

dead muerto *[mwairto]*

deaf sordo

deaf-aid un aparato del oído *[o-eedo]*

deal (*business*) una transacción *[—akth-yon]*; **it's a deal** trato hecho *[aycho]*; **will you deal with it?** ¿puede usted ocuparse de ello? *[pway-day oostay okoopar-say day eyo]*

dealer (*agent*) un distribuidor *[deestree-bweedor]*

dear querido *[kaireedo]*; (*expensive*) caro; **Dear Sir** muy señor mío *[mwee]*; **Dear Madam** estimada señora; **Dear Francisco** querido Francisco

death la muerte *[mwairtay]*

decadent decadente

December diciembre *[deeth-yembray]*

decent: that's very decent of you es usted muy amable *[mwee amablay]*

decide: we haven't decided yet todavía no hemos decidido *[aymos detheedeedo]*; **you decide for us** decida usted *[detheeda oostay]*; **it's all decided** está todo decidido

decision una decisión *[dethees-yon]*

deck la cubierta *[koob-yairta]*

deckchair una tumbona *[toombona]*

declare: I have nothing to declare no tengo nada que declarar *[... kay ...]*

decoration la decoración *[dekorath-yon]*

deduct descontar

deep profundo *[—oondo]*; **is it deep?** ¿es muy profundo? *[... mwee ...]*

deep-freeze un congelador *[kon-неlador]*

definitely ¡desde luego!; **definitely not** desde luego que no *[dezday lway-go kay no]*

degree (*university*) un título universitario *[teetoolo ooneebairseetar-yo]*; (*temperature*) un grado

dehydrated (*person*) deshidratado *[desee—]*

delay: the flight was delayed se retrasó el vuelo *[bwaylo]*

deliberately a propósito

delicacy: a local delicacy una especialidad local *[espeth-yaleeda]*

delicious delicioso *[deleeth-yoso]*

deliver: will you deliver it? ¿tienen servicio a domicilio? *[t-yenen sair-beeth-yo a domeetheel-yo]*

delivery: is there another mail delivery? ¿hay otro reparto de correo? *[eye ... korray-o]*

de luxe de lujo *[day loo-нo]*

denims unos vaqueros *[bakay-ros]*

Denmark Dinamarca

dent: there's a dent in it tiene una abolladura *[t-yenay oona aboyadoora]*

dental floss el hilo dental *[eelo]*

dentist un dentista

dentures la dentadura postiza *[pos-teetha]*

deny: he denies it lo niega *[n-yayga]*

deodorant un desodorante

department store unos grandes almacenes *[almathenays]*

departure la salida

departure lounge la sala de embarque *[embarkay]*

depend: it depends depende; **it depends on ...** depende de ...

deposit (*downpayment*) un depósito

depressed deprimido

depth la profundidad *[—foo—]*

description una descripción *[deskreepth-yon]*

deserted (*beach etc*) desierto *[des-yairto]*

dessert el postre

destination el destino

detergent un detergente *[detair-нentay]*

detour un rodeo *[roday-o]*

devalued devaluado *[debalwado]*

develop: could you develop these films? ¿puede revelar estos carretes? *[pway-day rebelar]*

diabetic diabético

diagram un esquema *[eskay-ma]*

dialect un dialecto *[d-yalekto]*

dialling code el prefijo *[prefee-нo]*

diamond un diamante *[d-yamantay]*

diaper un pañal *[pan-yal]*

diarrhoea, diarrhea diarrea *[d-yaray-a]*; **do you have something to stop diarrhoea?** ¿tiene algo para la diarrea? *[t-yenay]*

diary una agenda *[a-нenda]*
dictionary un diccionario *[deekth-yonar-yo]*; **a Spanish/English dictionary** un diccionario español/inglés
die morir; **I'm absolutely dying for a drink** me muero de sed *[may mwairo]*
didn't *see* **not** *and page 113*
diesel *(fuel)* el gas-oil
diet una dieta *[d-yayta]*; **I'm on a diet** estoy a dieta
difference la diferencia *[—th-ya]*; **what's the difference between ...?** ¿qué diferencia hay entre ...? *[... eye ...]*; **it doesn't make any difference** da lo mismo
different: they are different son diferentes; **they are very different** son muy distintos *[... mwee ...]*; **it's different from this one** es distinto de éste; **may we have a different table?** ¿pueden darnos otra mesa? *[pwayden]*; **ah well, that's different** bueno, eso es distinto
difficult difícil *[deefeetheel]*
difficulty la dificultad *[deefeekoolta]*; **without any difficulty** sin problemas; **I'm having difficulties with ...** tengo problemas con ...
digestion la digestión *[dee-нest-yon]*
dinghy un bote *[botay]*
dining car el vagón restaurante *[bagon rest-owrantay]*
dining room el comedor
dinner *(evening meal)* la cena *[thay-na]*
dinner jacket un smoking
dinner party una cena *[thay-na]*
dipped headlights las luces cortas *[loothes]*
dipstick la varilla graduada *[bareeya gradwada]*
direct directo; **does it go direct?** ¿va directo? *[ba]*
direction la dirección *[deerekth-yon]*; **in which direction is it?** ¿en qué dirección está?; **is it in this direction?** ¿es por aquí? *[akee]*
directory: telephone directory la guía telefónica *[g-ee-a]*; **directory enquiries** información *[eenformath-yon]*
dirt la suciedad *[sooth-yayda]*
dirty sucio *[sooth-yo]*
disabled minusválido *[meenoosbaleedo]*
disagree: it disagrees with me *(food)* no me sienta bien *[no may s-yenta b-yen]*

disappear desaparecer *[—ethair]*; **it's just disappeared** ha desaparecido *[—etheedo]*
disappointed: I was disappointed me decepcionó *[may dethepth-yono]*
disappointing decepcionante *[dethepth-yonantay]*
disaster un desastre
discharge *(medical)* el pus *[poos]*
disc: disc of film un disco para fotos
disc jockey un disc jockey
disco una discoteca
disco dancing: to go disco dancing ir a bailar a una discoteca *[... by-lar ...]*
discount un descuento *[deskwento]*
disease una enfermedad *[enfairmeda]*
disgusting repugnante
dish un plato
dishcloth un paño de cocina *[panyo day kotheena]*
dishonest poco honrado *[on—]*
dishwashing liquid un detergente lavavajillas *[detair-нentay laba-baнee-yas]*
disinfectant un desinfectante
dislocated shoulder un hombro dislocado *[ombro]*
dispensing chemist una farmacia *[farmath-ya]*
disposable nappies unos pañales braguita *[pan-yales brageeta]*
distance la distancia *[—th-ya]*; **what's the distance from ... to ...?** ¿qué distancia hay entre ... y ...? *[kay ... eye ...]*; **in the distance** a lo lejos *[lay-нos]*
distilled water agua destilada
distributor *(car)* el distribuidor
disturb: the disco is disturbing us la discoteca nos molesta
diversion un desvío *[dezbee-o]*
diving board un trampolín
divorced divorciado *[deeborth-yado]*
dizzy *(feel)* mareado *[maray-ado]*; **dizzy spells** unos mareos *[maray-os]*
do hacer *[ath-air]*; **what shall I do?** ¿qué hago? *[kay ago]*; **what are you doing tonight?** ¿qué vas a hacer esta noche? *[kay bas athair]*; **how do you do it?** ¿cómo se hace? *[say athay]*; **will you do it for me?** ¿me lo quiere hacer usted? *[k-yairay athair oostay]*; **who did it?** ¿quién lo hizo? *[k-yen lo eetho]*; **the meat's not done** la carne no está bien

hecha *[b-yen aycha]*; **do you have ...?** ¿tiene ...? *[t-yenay]*; **what do you do?** ¿en qué trabaja? *[en kay traba-нa]*

docks el puerto *[pwairto]*

doctor el médico; **he needs a doctor** necesita un médico *[netheseeta]*; **can you call a doctor?** ¿puede llamar a un médico? *[pway-day yamar]*

document un documento *[dokoomento]*

dog un perro

doll una muñeca *[moon-yayka]*

dollar un dólar

donkey un burro

don't! ¡no lo haga! *[aga] see pages 113, 114*

door una puerta *[pwairta]*

doorman el portero

dormobile (*tm*) una caravana *[—bana]*

dosage una dosis *[dosees]*

double: double room una habitación doble *[abeetath-yon doblay]*; **double bed** una cama de matrimonio; **double brandy** un coñac doble; **double r** (*in spelling name*) erre doble; **it's all double dutch to me** eso me suena a chino *[may swayna a cheeno]*

doubt: I doubt it lo dudo *[doodo]*

douche una ducha *[doocha]*

doughnut un dónut *[donoot]*

down: get down! ¡baje! *[ba-нay]*; **he's not down yet** (*out of bed*) todavía no se ha levantado *[lebantado]*; **further down the road** más adelante; **I paid 20% down** he pagado el 20% de depósito

downmarket (*restaurant etc*) barato

downstairs abajo *[aba-нo]*

dozen una docena *[dothay-na]*; **half a dozen** media docena *[mayd-ya]*

drain un desagüe *[desag-way]*

draughts (*game*) (juego de) damas *[н-waygo]*

draughty: it's rather draughty hay mucha corriente *[korr-yentay]*

drawing pin una chincheta *[cheenchayta]*

dreadful horrible *[orreeblay]*

dream un sueño *[sway-nyo]*; **it's like a bad dream** es como una pesadilla *[—eeya]*; **sweet dreams** ¡que duermas bien! *[kay dwairmas b-yen]*

dress (*woman's*) un vestido *[besteedo]*; **I'll just get dressed** voy a vestirme enseguida *[besteermay enseg-eeda]*

dressing (*for wound*) un vendaje *[benda-*

нay]*; (*for salad*) el aliño *[aleen-yo]*

dressing gown una bata

drink (*verb*) beber *[bebair]*; (*alcoholic*) una copa; **can I get you a drink?** ¿quiere beber algo? *[ky-airay]*; **I don't drink** no bebo *[baybo]*; **a long cool drink** un refresco; **may I have a drink of water?** ¿puede darme un vaso de agua? *[pway-day darmay oom baso day agwa]*; **drink up!** ¡bébetelo! *[bebay-taylo]*; **I had too much to drink** he bebido demasiado *[ay]*

drinkable potable *[potablay]*

drive: we drove here vinimos en coche *[beeneemos en ko-chay]*; **I'll drive you home** te llevaré a casa en el coche *[tay yay-baray]*; **do you want to come for a drive?** ¿quiere venir a dar una vuelta conmigo en el coche? *[k-yairay beneer a dar oona bwelta]*; **is it a very long drive?** ¿es un viaje muy largo? *[es oom b-yaнay mwee largo]*; **can you drive?** ¿sabe conducir? *[kondootheer]*

driver el conductor *[kondooktor]*

driver's license el permiso de conducir *[kondoo-theer]*

drive shaft el eje de transmisión *[e-нay day transmees-yon]*

driving licence el permiso de conducir *[kondoo-theer]*

drizzle: it's drizzling está lloviznando *[yobeethnando]*

drop: just a drop un poquito *[pokeeto]*; **I dropped it** se me cayó *[say may ka-yo]*; **drop in some time** ven a vernos alguna vez *[ben a bair-nos algoona beth]*

drown: he's drowning se está ahogando *[say esta a-o-gando]*

drug una droga; (*medicine*) un medicamento

drugstore una farmacia *[farmath-ya]*

drunk borracho

drunken driving conducir en estado de embriaguez *[kondootheer ... embryageth]*

dry seco

dry-clean limpieza en seco *[leemp-yaytha]*

dry-cleaner una tintorería

duck un pato

due: when is the bus due? ¿a qué hora debe llegar el autobús? *[a kay ora debay yay-gar el ow-toboos]*

dumb mudo *[moodo]*; (*stupid*) estúpido *[estoo—]*
dummy (*for baby*) un chupete *[choo-paytay]*
durex (*tm*) un preservativo *[presairbateebo]*
during durante *[doorantay]*
dust el polvo *[polbo]*

dustbin el cubo de la basura *[koobo]*
duster un trapo del polvo
Dutch holandés *[olandays]*
duty-free (*goods*) libre de impuestos *[eempwestos]*
duvet un edredón
dynamo la dínamo *[deenamo]*
dysentery la disentería

E

each: each of them cada uno de ellos *[eyos]*; **one for each of us** uno para cada uno; **how much are they each?** ¿cuánto es cada uno? *[kwanto]*; **each time** cada vez *[beth]*; **we know each other** nos conocemos *[konothaymos]*
ear la oreja *[oray-нa]*
earache el dolor de oídos *[o-eedos]*
early temprano; **early in the morning** por la mañana temprano; **it's too early** es demasiado temprano; **a day earlier** un día antes; **half an hour earlier** media hora antes *[mayd-ya ora]*; **I need an early night** necesito irme a la cama temprano *[netheseeto]*
early riser: I'm an early riser me gusta levantarme temprano *[lebantarmay]*
earring un pendiente *[pend-yentay]*
earth (*soil*) la tierra *[t-yairra]*
earthenware cacharros de barro
earwig una tijereta *[tee-нairayta]*
east este; **to the east** al este
Easter la Semana Santa
easy fácil *[fatheel]*; **easy with the cream!** ¡no tanta nata!
eat comer *[komair]*; **something to eat** algo de comer; **we've already eaten** ya hemos comido *[ya aymos]*
eau-de-Cologne agua de colonia *[agwa]*
eccentric excéntrico *[esth—]*
edible comestible *[—eeblay]*
efficient (*staff etc*) eficiente *[efeeth-yentay]*
egg un huevo *[way-bo]*
eggplant una berenjena *[bairen-нayna]*

Eire Eire *[airay]*
either: either ... or ... o ... o ...; **I don't like either of them** no me gusta ninguno de ellos *[neengoono day eyos]*; **either will do** me gustan los dos *[goostan]*
elastic elástico
elastic band una gomita
Elastoplast las tiritas
elbow el codo
electric eléctrico
electric blanket una manta eléctrica
electric cooker una cocina eléctrica *[kotheena]*
electric fire una estufa eléctrica *[estoofa]*
electrician un electricista *[—eetheesta]*
electricity la electricidad *[elektreetheeda]*
electric outlet un enchufe *[enchoofay]*
elegant elegante
elevator el ascensor *[asthensor]*
else: something else algo más; **somewhere else** en otra parte; **let's go somewhere else** vamos a otra parte *[bamos]*; **what else?** ¿qué más?; **nothing else, thanks** nada más, gracias; **is there anywhere else to go?** ¿hay algún otro sitio para ir? *[eye]*
embarrassed avergonzado *[abairgonthado]*
embarrassing violento *[b-yolento]*
embassy la embajada *[embaнada]*
emergency una emergencia *[emair-нenth-ya]*; **this is an emergency** es una emergencia
emery board lima de uñas *[oon-yas]*

emotional (*person*) sentimental
empty vacío [*bathee-o*]
end el final; **at the end of the road** al final de la calle [*ka-yay*]; **when does it end?** ¿cuándo termina? [*kwando*]
energetic activo [*akteebo*]
energy la energía [*enair-нee-a*]
engaged (*toilet*) ocupado [*okoopado*]; (*telephone*) comunicando; [*komoonee-kando*]; (*person*) prometido
engagement ring el anillo de prometida [*anee-yo*]
engine el motor
engine trouble problemas con el motor
England Inglaterra
English inglés [*eenglays*]; **the English** los ingleses [*eenglay-says*]; **I'm English** soy inglés/inglesa
Englishman un inglés [*eenglays*]
English woman una inglesa [*eenglaysa*]
enjoy: I enjoyed it very much me gustó mucho [*may goosto moocho*]; **enjoy yourself!** ¡que se divierta! [*kay say deeb-yairta*]
enjoyable entretenido
enlargement (*of photo*) una ampliación [*ampl-yath-yon*]
enormous enorme [*enormay*]
enough suficiente [*soofeeth-yentay*]; **there's not enough ...** no hay bastante; **it's not big enough** no es suficientemente grande; **thank you, that's enough** gracias, es suficiente
entertainment las diversiones [*deebairs-yones*]
enthusiastic entusiasta
entrance la entrada
envelope un sobre [*sobray*]
epileptic epiléptico
equipment el equipo [*ekeepo*]; (*in apartment*) los utensilios [*ootenseel-yos*]
eraser una goma
erotic erótico
error un error
escalator una escalera mecánica
especially especialmente [*espeth-yalmentay*]
espresso (coffee) un (café) expreso
essential imprescindible [*eemprestheen-deeblay*]; **it is essential that ...** es necesario que ... [*es nethesar-yo kay*]
estate agent un agente inmobiliario [*a-нentay*]

ethnic (*restaurant*) típico español
Eurocheque un eurocheque [*ay-ooroche-kay*]
Eurocheque card una tarjeta eurocheque [*tar-нayta*]
Europe Europa [*ay-ooro-pa*]
European europeo [*ay-ooropayo*]
European plan media pensión [*mayd-ya pens-yon*]
even: even the Spanish hasta los españoles [*asta*]; **even if ...** incluso si ... [*eenklooso*]
evening la tarde [*tarday*]; (*after nightfall*) la noche [*notchay*]; **good evening** buenas tardes [*bwenas*]; **this evening** esta tarde/noche; **in the evening** por la tarde/noche; **evening meal** la cena [*thayna*]
evening dress traje de etiqueta [*tra-нay day eteekay-ta*]; (*woman's*) un traje de noche
eventually finalmente
ever: have you ever been to ...? ¿ha estado alguna vez en ...? [*a estado algoo-na beth en*]; **if you ever come to Britain** si alguna vez viene a Gran Bretaña [*... beth b-yenay ...*]
every cada; **every day** todos los días
everyone todos
everything todo
everywhere en todas partes
exact exacto
exactly! ¡exactamente!
exam un examen
example un ejemplo [*eнemplo*]; **for example** por ejemplo
excellent excelente [*esthelentay*]
except excepto [*esthepto*]; **except Sunday** excepto los domingos
exception una excepción [*esthepth-yon*]; **as an exception** como una excepción
excess exceso [*estheso*]
excess baggage exceso de equipaje [*estheso day ekeepa-нay*]
excessive (*bill etc*) excesivo [*estheseebo*]; **that's a bit excessive** es un poco excesivo
exchange (*money*) cambio; (*telephone*) la Central Telefónica [*thentral*]; **in exchange** a cambio
exchange rate: what's the exchange rate for the pound/dollar? ¿a cuánto está la libra/el dólar? [*kwanto*]
exciting emocionante [*emoth-yonantay*]

exclusive (*club etc*) selecto
excursion una excursión [*eskoors-yon*]; **is there an excursion to ...?** ¿hay una excursión a ...? [*eye*]
excuse me (*to get past etc*) con permiso [*pairmeeso*]; (*to get attention*) ¡por favor! [*fabor*]; (*apology*) perdone [*pairdonay*]
exhaust (*car*) el tubo de escape [*toobo day eskapay*]
exhausted agotado
exhibition una exposición [*esposeethyon*]
exist: does it still exist? ¿existe todavía?
exit la salida
expect: I expect so espero que sí; **she's expecting** está esperando un niño [*neenyo*]
expensive caro
experience: an unforgettable experience una experiencia inolvidable [*espairyenth-ya eenolbeedablay*]
experienced con experiencia [*espairyenth-ya*]
expert un experto [*espairto*]
expire: it's expired está caducado
explain explicar [*espleekar*]; **would you explain that to me?** ¿puede explicármelo? [*pway-day*]
explore explorar; **I just want to go and explore** sólo quiero ir a ver [*k-yairo eer a bair*]
export la exportación [*esportath-yon*]
exposure meter el fotómetro
express (*mail*) urgente [*oor-нentay*]
extra: can we have an extra chair? ¿puede traernos otra silla? [*pway-day tra-airnos otra see-ya*]; **is that extra?** ¿es eso extra?
extraordinary extraordinario [*estra—*]
extremely sumamente [*soomamentay*]
extrovert un extrovertido [*estrobairteedo*]
eye un ojo [*oнo*]; **will you keep an eye on it for me?** ¿puede cuidármelo? [*pway-day kweedarmaylo*]
eye drops gotas para los ojos [*o-нos*]
eyebrow una ceja [*thay-нa*]
eyebrow pencil lápiz de cejas [*lapeeth day thay-нas*]
eyeliner un lápiz de ojos [*lapeeth day o-нos*]
eye shadow una sombra de ojos [*oнos*]
eye witness un testigo presencial [*presenth-yal*]

F

fabulous fabuloso [*fabooloso*]
face la cara
face mask unas gafas de bucear [*day boothay-ar*]
face pack mascarilla de belleza [*maskaree-ya day be-yaytha*]
facing: facing the sea enfrente del mar
fact un hecho [*aycho*]
factory una fábrica
Fahrenheit *see page 119*
faint: she's fainted se ha desmayado [*say a desma-yado*]; **I think I'm going to faint** creo que me voy a desmayar [*kray-o kay may boy a desma-yar*]
fair (*fun-*) las ferias [*fair-yas*]; **it's not fair** no es justo [*нoosto*];

fair enough muy bien [*mwee b-yen*]
fake una falsificación [*falseefeekath-yon*]
fall: he's had a fall se ha caído [*say a ka-eedo*]; **he fell off his bike** se ha caído de la bicicleta [*beetheeklayta*]; (*season*) la primavera [*—baira*]
false falso [*fal-so*]
false teeth los dientes postizos [*d-yentays posteethos*]
family la familia [*fameel-ya*]
family hotel un hotel familiar [*otel*]
family name el apellido [*a-pe-yeedo*]
famished: I'm famished me muero de hambre [*may mwairo day ambray*]
famous famoso
fan (*mechanical*) un ventilador [*benteela-*

dor]; (*hand held*) un abanico; (*pop etc*) un fan; (*football*) un hincha *[eencha]*
fan belt la correa del ventilador *[korray-a del ben—]*
fancy: he fancies you le gustas *[lay goostas]*
fancy dress un disfraz *[deesfrath]*
fantastic fantástico
far lejos *[lay-HOS]*; **is it far?** ¿está lejos?; **how far is it to ...?** ¿cuánto hay de aquí a ...? *[kwanto eye day akee]*; **as far as I'm concerned** en lo que a mí respecta
fare: what's the fare to ...? ¿cuánto cuesta el billete para ...? *[kwanto kwesta el beeyay-tay]*
farewell party una fiesta de despedida
farm una granja *[gran-Ha]*
farther más allá *[a-ya]*; **farther than ...** más allá de ...
fashion la moda
fashionable de moda
fast rápido; **not so fast** no tan de prisa
fastener (*on clothes*) un broche *[brochay]*
fat (*adjective*) gordo; (*on meat*) la grasa
father: my father mi padre *[mee padray]*
father-in-law el suegro *[swaygro]*
fathom una braza *[bratha]*
fattening: it's fattening engorda
faucet el grifo
fault un defecto; **it was my fault** fue culpa mía *[fway koolpa mee-a]*; **it's not my fault** no es culpa mía *[koolpa mee-a]*
faulty defectuoso
favo(u)rite favorito *[faboreeto]*; **that's my favourite** es mi preferido
fawn (*colour*) beige
February febrero
fed up: I'm fed up! ¡estoy harto! *[arto]*; **I'm fed up with ...** estoy harto de ...
feeding bottle un biberón
feel: I feel hot/cold tengo calor/frío; **I feel like a drink** me apetece algo de beber *[may a-petethay]*; **I don't feel like it** no me apetece; **how are you feeling today?** ¿qué tal se encuentra hoy? *[kay tal say enkwentra oy]*; **I'm feeling a lot better** me encuentro mucho mejor *[may enkwentro moocho meHor]*
felt-tip (pen) un rotulador
fence una valla *[ba-ya]*
ferry el ferry; **what time's the last ferry?** ¿a qué hora es el último ferry? *[a kay ora]*
festival un festival *[—bal]*

fetch: I'll go and fetch it voy a buscarlo *[boy]*; **will you come and fetch me?** ¿quiere venir a buscarme? *[k-yairay beneer a booskar-may]*
fever la fiebre *[f-yaybray]*
feverish: I'm feeling feverish tengo fiebre *[f-yaybray]*
few: only a few sólo unos pocos; **a few minutes** unos minutos; **he's had a good few (to drink)** ha tomado unas cuantas de más *[... kwantas ...]*
fiancé: my fiancé mi novio *[mee nob-yo]*
fiancée: my fiancée mi novia *[mee nob-ya]*
fiasco: what a fiasco! ¡qué desastre! *[kay]*
field un campo
fifty-fifty a medias *[mayd-yas]*
fight una pelea *[pelay-a]*
figs unos higos *[eegos]*
figure una figura *[feegoora]*; (*number*) una cifra *[theefra]*; **I have to watch my figure** tengo que guardar la línea *[gwardar la leenay-a]*
fill llenar *[yaynar]*; **fill her up please** lleno, por favor *[yayno]*; **will you help me fill out this form?** ¿puede ayudarme a rellenar este impreso? *[pway-day ayoodarmay a ray-yaynar]*
fillet un filete
filling (*tooth*) un empaste *[empastay]*; **it's very filling** llena mucho *[yayna]*
filling station una gasolinera
film (*phot, movie*) una película; **do you have this type of film?** ¿tiene películas de este tipo? *[t-yenay peleekoolas]*; **16mm film** un carrete de 16mm; **35mm film** un carrete de 35mm; **film processing** el revelado de películas *[rebelado]*
filter un filtro
filter-tipped con filtro
filthy sucísimo *[sootheeseemo]*
find encontrar; **I can't find it** no puedo encontrarlo *[no pway-do]*; **if you find it** si lo encuentra *[enkwentra]*; **I've found a ...** he encontrado un ... *[ay]*
fine: it's fine weather hace buen tiempo *[athay bwen t-yempo]*; **a 3,000 peseta fine** una multa de tres mil pesetas *[moolta]*; **thank you, that's fine** (*to waiter etc*) está bien, gracias *[b-yen]*; **how are you? — fine thanks** ¿cómo está? —

bien, gracias

finger un dedo

fingernail una uña *[ooñ-ya]*

finish: I haven't finished no he terminado *[no ay tairmeenado]*; **when I've finished** cuando acabe *[kwando akabay]*; **when does it finish?** ¿cuándo termina? *[kwando]*; **finish off your drink** acabe la bebida *[akabay]*

Finland Finlandia

fire: fire! ¡fuego! *[fway-go]*; **may we light a fire here?** ¿se puede encender fuego aquí? *[say pway-day enthen-dair fwaygo akee]*; **it's on fire** está ardiendo *[ardyendo]*; **it's not firing properly** el encendido no funciona bien *[el enthendeedo no foonth-yona b-yen]*

fire alarm la alarma de incendios *[eenthend-yos]*

fire brigade, fire department los bomberos

fire escape la salida de incendios *[eenthend-yos]*

fire extinguisher un extintor *[esteentor]*

firm *(company)* una compañía *[kompanyee-a]*

first primero *[preemairo]*; **I was first** yo soy el primero; **at first** al principio *[preentheep-yo]*; **this is the first time that ...** es la primera vez que ... *[... beth ...]*

first aid primeros auxilios *[preemairos owkseel-yos]*

first aid kit un botiquín *[boteekeen]*

first class *(travel)* primera (clase) *[preemaira]*

first name el nombre de pila

fish un pez *[peth]*; *(to eat)* pescado

fisherman un pescador

fishing la pesca

fishing boat un barco de pesca

fishing net una red de pesca

fishing rod una caña de pescar *[kan-ya]*

fishing tackle el aparejo de pesca *[aparay-но]*

fishing village un pueblo de pescadores *[pweblo]*

fit *(healthy)* en forma; **I'm not very fit** no estoy en forma; **a keep fit fanatic** un fanático del keep fit; **it doesn't fit** no me vale *[balay]*

fix: can you fix it? *(arrange, repair)* ¿puede arreglarlo? *[pway-day]*; **let's fix a time** fijemos una hora *[fee-наymos oona ora]*;

it's all fixed up todo está arreglado; **I'm in a bit of a fix** estoy en un aprieto *[apr-yayto]*

fizzy con gas

fizzy drink una bebida gaseosa *[gassayosa]*

flab *(on body)* la grasa

flag una bandera

flannel *(for washing)* una manopla

flash *(phot)* un flash

flashcube un flashcube

flashlight una linterna *[leentairna]*

flashy *(clothes)* llamativo *[yamateebo]*

flat *(adjective)* llano *[yano]*; **this beer is flat** esta cerveza no tiene gas *[thairbaytha no t-yaynay]*; **I've got a flat (tyre)** tengo un pinchazo *[peenchatho]*; *(apartment)* un piso

flatterer un adulador

flatware *(cutlery)* los cubiertos *[koob yairtos]*; *(plates)* la loza *[lotha]*

flavo(u)r el sabor

flea una pulga *[poolga]*

flea powder un insecticida para las pulgas *[—eetheeda]*

flexible flexible *[—eeblay]*

flies *(on trousers)* la bragueta *[bragayta]*

flight el vuelo *[bwaylo]*

flippers las aletas

flirt coquetear *[kok-etay-ar]*

float flotar

flood una inundación *[eenoondath-yon]*

floor *(of room)* el suelo *[swaylo]*; *(storey)* el piso; **on the floor** en el suelo; **on the second floor** *(UK)* en el segundo piso; *(USA)* en el primer piso

floorshow un espectáculo

flop *(failure)* un fracaso

florist una floristería

flour la harina *[areena]*

flower una flor

flu la gripe *[greepay]*

fluent: he speaks fluent Spanish habla muy buen castellano *[abla mwee bwen kasteyano]*

fly volar *[bolar]*; **can we fly to ...?** ¿podemos ir en avión a ...? *[ab-yon]*

fly *(insect)* una mosca

fly spray un spray matamoscas *[espry]*

foggy: it's foggy hay niebla *[eye n-yaybla]*

fog light un faro antiniebla *[anteen-yaybla]*

folk dance un baile regional [*by-lay reн-yonal*]

folk music la música folklórica [*mooseeka fol-kloreeka*]

follow seguir [*seg-eer*]; **follow me** sígame [*seegamay*]

fond: I'm quite fond of ... me gusta mucho el/la ... [*may goosta*]

food la comida; **the food's excellent** la comida es excelente [*esthelentay*]

food poisoning una intoxicación alimenticia [*eentoxeekath-yon aleementeeth-ya*]

food store una tienda de comestibles [*t-yenda day komesteeblays*]

fool un tonto

foolish tonto

foot un pie [*p-yay*]; **on foot** a pie

football el fútbol; (*ball*) un balón

for: is that for me? ¿es eso para mí?; **what's this for?** ¿para qué es esto?; **for two days** (*rent etc*) para dos días; **I've been here for a week** he estado aquí una semana [*ay estado akee*]; **a bus for ...** un autobús para ... [*owtoboos*]

forbidden prohibido [*pro-eebee-do*]

forehead la frente

foreign extranjero [*estran-нairo*]

foreigner un extranjero [*estran-нairo*]

foreign exchange las divisas [*deebeesas*]

forest un bosque [*boskay*]

forget olvidar [*olbeedar*]; **I forget, I've forgotten** no me acuerdo, me he olvidado [*no may akwairdo may ay olbeedado*]; **don't forget** no se olvide [*olbeeday*]

fork un tenedor; (*in road*) una bifurcación [*beefoorkath-yon*]

form (*document*) un impreso

formal (*person*) estirado; (*dress*) de etiqueta [*eteekay-ta*]

fortnight quince días [*keen-thay*]

fortunately afortunadamente

fortune-teller un adivino [*adeebeeno*]

forward: could you forward my mail? ¿puede enviarme el correo a mi nueva dirección? [*pway-day emb-yarmay el korray-o a mee nwayba deerekth-yon*]

forwarding address la nueva dirección [*nwayba deerekth-yon*]

foundation cream una crema base [*bassay*]

fountain una fuente [*fwentay*]

foyer (*of theatre etc*) el hall

fracture una fractura [*—oora*]

fractured skull una fractura de cráneo [*kranay-o*]

fragile frágil [*fra-нeel*]

frame (*picture*) un marco

France Francia [*franth-ya*]

fraud un fraude [*frowday*]

free libre [*leebray*]; **admission free** entrada gratis [*gratees*]

freezer un congelador [*kon-нelador*]

freezing cold frío glacial [*glath-yal*]

French francés [*franthays*]

French fries unas patatas fritas

Frenchman un francés [*franthays*]

Frenchwoman una francesa [*franthaysa*]

frequent frecuente [*fray-kwentay*]

fresh fresco; **don't get fresh with me** no sea fresco (conmigo) [*no say-a*]; **I want some fresh air** quiero respirar aire puro [*k-yairo respeerar eye-ray pooro*]

fresh orange juice un zumo de naranja natural [*thoomo de naran-нa natooral*]

friction tape una cinta aislante [*theenta eye-slantay*]

Friday viernes [*b-yairnays*]

fridge el frigorífico

fried egg un huevo frito [*waybo*]

friend un amigo

friendly simpático

frog una rana

from: I'm from London soy de Londres [*soy day londrays*]; **from here to the beach** de aquí a la playa [*day akee*]; **the next boat from ...** el próximo barco de ...; **as from Tuesday** desde el martes [*dez-day*]

front la parte delantera [*—taira*]; **in front** delante; **in front of us** delante de nosotros; **at the front** por delante

frost la escarcha

frozen congelado [*kon-нaylado*]

frozen food congelados [*kon-нaylados*]

fruit fruta [*froota*]

fruit juice un zumo de frutas [*thoomo*]

fruit machine una máquina tragaperras [*makeena*]

fruit salad una macedonia de frutas [*math-edon-ya*]

frustrating: it's very frustrating es muy frustrante [*mwee froostrantay*]

fry freír [*fray-eer*]; **nothing fried** nada

frito

frying pan una sartén

full lleno *[yayno]*; **it's full of ...** está lleno de ...; **I'm full** estoy lleno

full-board pensión completa *[pens-yon]*

full-bodied (*wine*) con cuerpo *[kwairpo]*

fun: it's fun es divertido *[deebairteedo]*; **it was great fun** fue muy divertido *[fway mwee deebairteedo]*; **just for fun** en broma; **have fun!** ¡que se divierta! *[kay say deeb-yairta]*

funeral un funeral *[foonairal]*

funny (*strange*) raro *[ra-ro]*; (*comical*) gracioso *[grath-yoso]*

furniture los muebles *[mway-blays]*

further más allá *[a-ya]*; **2 kilometres further** 2 kilómetros más allá; **further down the road** más adelante

fuse el fusible *[fooseeblay]*; **the lights have fused** se fundieron los plomos *[say foond-yayron]*

fuse wire un plomo

future futuro *[footoo-ro]*; **in future** en lo sucesivo *[sooth-eseebo]*

G

gale un vendaval *[bendabal]*

gallon un galón *see page 119*

gallstone un cálculo biliario *[kalkoolo beel-yar-yo]*

gamble jugar *[Hoogar]*; **I don't gamble** nunca juego *[—Hway-go]*

game (*sport*) el partido

games room la sala de juegos *[Hwaygos]*

gammon jamón ahumado *[Hamon a-oomado]*

garage (*repair*) un taller de reparaciones *[ta-yair day reparath-yonays]*; (*fuel*) una gasolinera *[—eenaira]*; (*parking*) un garaje *[gara-Hay]*

garbage la basura *[basoora]*

garden el jardín *[Hardeen]*

garlic el ajo *[a-Ho]*

gas el gas; (*for car*) la gasolina

gas cylinder una bombona de gas

gas permeable lenses unas lentillas porosas *[lentee-yas]*

gasket una junta *[Hoonta]*

gas pedal el acelerador *[athelairador]*

gas station una gasolinera

gas tank el depósito de gasolina

gastro-enteritis gastroenteritis

gate la puerta *[pwairta]*

gauge el indicador del nivel *[neebel]*

gay (*homosexual*) un marica *[mareeka]*

gear (*car*) la marcha; (*equipment*) el equipo *[ekeepo]*; **the gears stick** los cambios se traban

gearbox: I have gearbox trouble le pasa algo a la caja de cambios *[ka-Ha day kamb-yos]*

gear lever, gear shift la palanca de velocidades *[belotheedadays]*

general delivery la lista de correos *[korray-os]*

generous: that's very generous of you es muy amable *[mwee amablay]*

gentleman: that gentleman over there el señor de allá *[aya]*; **he's such a gentleman** es tan educado *[edookado]*

gents los aseos *[assay-os]*

genuine (*antique etc*) genuino *[Hen-weeno]*

German alemán *[alayman]*

German measles la rubéola *[roobay-ola]*

Germany Alemania *[alayman-ya]*

get: have you got ...? ¿tiene usted ...? *[t-yenay oostay]*; **how do I get to ...?** ¿podría decirme cómo llegar a ...? *[podree-a detheermay komo yaygar]*; **where do I get them from?** ¿dónde puedo conseguirlos ...? *[donday pway-do konsegeerlos]*; **can I get you a drink?** ¿puedo ofrecerle algo de beber? *[pway-do ofrethair-lay]*; **will you get it for me?** ¿me lo podría traer? *[may lo podree-a tra-air]*; **when do we get there?** ¿cuándo llegamos? *[kwando yay-gamos]*; **I've got to go** tengo que marcharme; **where do I**

get off? ¿dónde tengo que bajarme? *[baнarmay]*; **it's difficult to get to ...** es difícil llegar a ... *[deefeetheel yaygar]*; **when I get up** (*in morning*) cuando me levanto *[kwando may lebanto]*

ghastly horrible *[orreeblay]*

ghost un fantasma

Gibraltar Gibraltar *[нeebraltar]*

Gibraltarian gibraltareño *[нeebraltarayn-yo]*

giddy: it makes me giddy me marea *[maray-a]*

gift un regalo

gigantic gigantesco *[нee—]*

gin ginebra *[нeenaybra]*; **a gin and tonic** una tónica con ginebra

girl una chica

girlfriend (*general*) una amiga; (*sweetheart*) la novia *[nob-ya]*

give dar; **will you give me ...?** ¿me quiere dar ...? *[may k-yairay]*; **I gave it to him** se lo di a él *[... dee ...]*; **I'll give you 300 pesetas** le daré trescientas pesetas *[lay daray]*; **will you give it back?** ¿lo va a devolver? *[lo ba a day-bolbair]*; **would you give this to ...?** ¿podría entregarle esto a ...? *[podree-a]*

glad alegre *[a-legray]*; **I'm so glad** estoy tan contento

glamorous muy atractiva *[mwee atrakteeba]*

gland una glándula *[glandoola]*

glandular fever fiebre glandular *[fyaybray glandoolar]*

glass (*substance*) el cristal *[kreestal]*; (*drinking*) un vaso *[basso]*; **a glass of water** un vaso de agua *[agwa]*

glasses las gafas

gloves los guantes *[gwantays]*

glue goma (de pegar)

gnat un mosquito

go ir *[eer]*; **we want to go to ...** queremos ir a ...; **I'm going there tomorrow** mañana iré allí *[iray ayee]*; **when does it go?** (*leave*) ¿a qué hora sale? *[a kay ora salay]*; **where are you going?** ¿adónde va? *[adonday ba]*; **let's go** vámonos *[bamonos]*; **he's gone** (*left*) se ha marchado; **it's all gone** se ha acabado; **I went there yesterday** fui allí ayer *[fwee ayee ayair]*; **a hotdog to go** (*to take away*) un perro caliente para llevar *[yaybar]*; **go away!** ¡váyase! *[baya-say]*; **it's gone off** (*food*)

la comida está pasada; **we're going out tonight** vamos a salir esta noche *[bamos]*; **do you want to go out tonight?** ¿quiere salir esta noche? *[k-yairay]*; **has the price gone up?** ¿ha subido el precio? *[preth-yo]*

goal (*sport*) un gol

goat una cabra

goat's cheese queso de cabra *[kay-so]*

God Dios *[d-yos]*

gold el oro

golf el golf

golf clubs los palos de golf

golf course el campo de golf

good bueno *[bweno]*; **good!** ¡muy bien! *[mwee b-yen]*; **that's no good** eso no sirve *[seerbay]*; **good heavens!** ¡cielos! *[th-yaylos]*

goodbye adiós *[ad-yos]*

good-looking guapo *[gwapo]*

gooey (*food etc*) viscoso

goose un ganso

gooseberries grosellas *[gro-se-yas]*

gorgeous magnífico

gourmet un gastrónomo

gourmet food comidas gastronómicas

government el gobierno *[gob-yairno]*

gradually gradualmente *[grad-wal—]*

grammar la gramática

gram(me) un gramo

granddaughter la nieta *[n-yayta]*

grandfather el abuelo *[abwaylo]*

grandmother la abuela *[abwayla]*

grandson el nieto *[n-yayto]*

grapefruit un pomelo

grapefruit juice un zumo de pomelo *[thoomo]*

grapes unas uvas *[oobas]*

grass la hierba *[yairba]*

grateful agradecido *[agradetheedo]*; **I'm very grateful to you** se lo agradezco mucho *[... agradeth-ko ...]*

gravy la salsa

gray gris

grease la grasa

greasy (*cooking*) grasiento

great grande; (*very good*) muy bueno *[mwee bweno]*; **that's great!** ¡estupendo!

Great Britain Gran Bretaña *[bretanya]*

Greece Grecia *[grayth-ya]*

greedy (*for food*) comilón

green verde *[bairday]*

green card (*insurance*) la carta verde

[bairday]
greengrocer (*shop*) la frutería
[frootairee-a]
grey gris
grilled a la parrilla *[pareeya]*
gristle (*on meat*) un nervio *[nairb-yo]*
grocer un ultramarinos *[ooltra—]*
ground el suelo *[swaylo]*; **on the ground** en el suelo; **on the ground floor** en la planta baja *[ba-нa]*
ground beef la carne picada *[karnay peekada]*
group un grupo
group insurance un seguro colectivo *[—eebo]*
group leader el jefe del grupo *[нefay]*
guarantee la garantía *[garantee-a]*; **is it**

guaranteed? ¿está garantizado? *[garanteethado]*
guardian (*of child*) el tutor *[too-tor]*
guest el invitado *[eembeetado]*
guesthouse una casa de huéspedes *[kasa day wespedays]*
guest room la habitación de huéspedes *[abeetath-yon day wespedays]*
guide (*tourist*) el guía *[g-ee-a]*
guidebook la guía *[g-ee-a]*
guilty culpable *[koolpablay]*
guitar una guitarra *[geetarra]*
gum (*in mouth*) la encía *[enthee-a]*
gun una pistola
gymnasium el gimnasio *[нeemnas-yo]*
gyn(a)ecologist un ginecólogo *[нeenekologo]*

H

hair el pelo
hairbrush un cepillo para el pelo *[thepeeyo]*
haircut un corte de pelo; **just an ordinary haircut please** córteme el pelo nada más, por favor
hairdresser el peluquero *[pelookairo]*
hairdryer un secador de pelo
hair foam una espuma moldeadora de pelo *[espooma molday-adora]*
hair gel un gel fijador de pelo *[нel fee-нador]*
hair grip una horquilla *[orkee-ya]*
hair lacquer una laca
half la mitad *[la meeta]*; **half an hour** una media hora *[maid-ya ora]*; **a half portion** una media porción *[porth-yon]*; **half a litre** un medio litro; **half as much** la mitad; **half as much again** la mitad otra vez *[beth] see page 116*
halfway: halfway to Madrid a medio camino de Madrid *[maid-yo kameeno]*
ham jamón de York *[нamon]*
hamburger una hamburguesa *[amboorgay-sa]*
hammer un martillo *[marteeyo]*

hand una mano; **will you give me a hand?** ¿me echa una mano? *[may aycha]*
handbag un bolso
hand baggage equipaje de mano *[ekeepaнay]*
handbrake el freno de mano
handkerchief un pañuelo *[pan-ywaylo]*
handle (*door*) la manilla *[manee-ya]*; (*cup*) el asa *[assa]*; **will you handle it?** ¿puede ocuparse de ello? *[pway-day okoopar-say day eyo]*
hand luggage equipaje de mano *[ekeepaнay]*
hand made hecho a mano *[aycho]*
handsome guapo *[gwapo]*
hanger (*for clothes*) una percha *[paircha]*
hangover una resaca; **I've got a terrible hangover** tengo una resaca terrible
happen suceder *[sooth-edair]*; **how did it happen?** ¿cómo pasó? *[passo]*; **what's happening** ¿qué pasa? *[kay]*; **it won't happen again** no volverá a pasar *[no bolbaira]*
happy contento; **we're not happy with the room** no estamos contentos con la habitación

harbo(u)r el puerto [*pwairto*]
hard duro [*dooro*]; (*difficult*) difícil [*dee-feetheel*]
hard-boiled egg un huevo duro [*waybo*]
hard lenses unas lentillas duras [*lentee-yas dooras*]
hardly: hardly ever casi nunca [*kassee*]
hardware store una ferretería
harm el daño [*danyo*]
hassle: it's too much hassle es demasiado problemático; **a hassle-free holiday** unas vacaciones sin problemas [*bakath-yonays*]
hat un sombrero
hatchback (*car*) (un coche) con puerta trasera [*pwairta trasaira*]
hate: I hate ... odio ... [*od-yo*]
have tener [*tenair*]; **do you have ...?** ¿tiene ...? [*t-yenay*]; **can I have some water?** ¿puede traerme un poco de agua? [*pway-day tra-airmay*]; **I have ...** tengo ...; **I don't have ...** no tengo ...; **can we have breakfast in our room?** ¿podríamos desayunar en la habitación? [*podree-amos desayoonar en la abeetath-yon*]; **have another** (*drink etc*) tome otro [*tomay*]; **I have to leave early** tengo que marcharme temprano; **do I have to ...?** ¿tengo que ...? *see page 109*
hay fever la fiebre del heno [*f-yaybray del ayno*]
he él; **has he come back yet?** ¿ha regresado ya? [*a*]; **where is he?** ¿dónde está?; **he's in his room** está en su habitación; **he's my brother** es mi hermano; **is he here?** ¿está (aquí)? [*akee*] *see page 105*
head la cabeza [*kabaytha*]; **we're heading for Madrid** nos dirigimos a Madrid [*deeree-Heemos*]
headache un dolor de cabeza [*kabaytha*]
headlight un faro
headphones los auriculares [*owreekoola-rays*]
head waiter el jefe de camareros [*Hefay*]
head wind un viento contrario [*b-yento kontrar-yo*]
health la salud [*saloo*]; **your health!** ¡a tu salud! [*a too*]
healthy sano
hear: can you hear me? ¿me oye? [*may oy-ay*]; **I can't hear you** no le oigo [*no lay oy-go*]; **I've heard about it** he oído hablar de eso [*ay o-eedo ablar*]

hearing aid un aparato del oído [*o-eedo*]
heart el corazón [*korathon*]
heart attack un infarto
heat el calor; **not in this heat!** ¡no con este calor!
heater (*in car*) la calefacción [*kalayfakth-yon*]
heating la calefacción [*kalayfakth-yon*]
heat rash el salpullido [*salpooyeedo*]
heat stroke una insolación [*insolath-yon*]
heatwave una ola de calor
heavy pesado
hectic agitado [*a-Heetado*]
heel (*of foot*) el talón; (*of shoe*) el tacón; **could you put new heels on these?** ¿podría cambiarles los tacones? [*podree-a kamb-yarlays*]
heelbar un zapatero [*thapatairo*]
height la altura [*altoora*]
helicopter un helicóptero
hell: oh hell! ¡diablos!; **go to hell!** ¡váyase al diablo! [*baya-say*]
hello! ¡hola! [*ola*]; (*on phone*) dígame [*deegamay*]
helmet (*motorcycle*) un casco
help ayudar [*ayoodar*]; **can you help me?** ¿puede ayudarme? [*pway-day ayoo-darmay*]; **thanks for your help** gracias por su ayuda; **help!** ¡socorro!
helpful: he was very helpful fue muy atento [*fway mwee*]; **that's helpful** es una gran ayuda
helping (*of food*) una porción [*porth-yon*]
hepatitis la hepatitis [*—teeteess*]
her: I don't know her no la conozco [*konothko*]; **will you send it to her?** ¿podría enviárselo a ella? [*emb-yarsay-lo*]; **it's her** es ella [*eya*]; **with her** con ella; **for her** para ella; **that's her suitcase** es su maleta *see pages 103, 105*
herbs hierbas [*yairbas*]
here aquí [*akee*]; **here you are** (*giving something*) tenga; **here he comes** aquí viene [*b-yenay*]
hers: that's hers es de ella, es suyo/suya *see page 107*
hey! ¡oiga!
hiccups el hipo [*eepo*]
hide esconder [*eskondair*]
hideous horrendo [*orrendo*]
high alto
highbeam las luces largas [*loothays*]
highchair (*for baby*) una silla alta [*seeya*]

highlighter el colorete

highway la autopista *[ow-topeesta]*

hiking excursionismo a pie *[eskoors-yo-neesmo a p-yay]*

hill una colina; **it's further up the hill** está más arriba en la colina

hilly accidentado *[aktheedentado]*

him: I don't know him no le conozco *[konothko]*; **will you send it to him?** ¿podría enviárselo a él? *[podree-a embyarsay-lo]*; **it's him** es él; **with him** con él *see page 105*

hip la cadera

hire: can I hire a car? ¿puedo alquilar un coche? *[pway-do alkeelar]*; **do you hire them out?** ¿los alquila? *[alkeela]*

his: it's his drink es su bebida; **it's his** es suyo/suya *[sooya] see pages 103, 107*

history: the history of Madrid la historia de Madrid *[eestorya]*

hit: he hit me me golpeó *[golpay-o]*; **I hit my head** me golpeé la cabeza *[golpay-ay]*

hitch: is there a hitch? ¿hay algún problema?

hitch-hike hacer autostop *[athair owtostop]*

hitch-hiker un autostopista *[owtostopeesta]*

hit record un disco de éxito *[eggs-eeto]*

Holland Holanda *[o—]*

hole un agujero *[agoo-нairo]*

holiday las vacaciones *[bakath-yonays]*; **I'm on holiday** estoy de vacaciones

home la casa; **at home** en casa; *(in my own country)* en mi país *[pa-ees]*; **I go home tomorrow** me marcho a casa mañana; **home sweet home!** ¡hogar, dulce hogar! *[ogar]*

home address el domicilio *[domeetheel-yo]*

homemade de fabricación casera *[fabreekath-yon kasaira]*

homesick: I'm homesick tengo morriña *[morreen-ya]*

honest honrado *[onrado]*

honestly? ¿de verdad? *[day bairda]*

honey la miel *[m-yel]*

honeymoon la luna de miel *[loona day m-yel]*; **it's our honeymoon** es nuestra luna de miel; **a second honeymoon** una segunda luna de miel

honeymoon suite la suite nupcial

[nooth-yal]

hoover *(tm)* una aspiradora

hope la esperanza *[—antha]*; **I hope so** espero que sí; **I hope not** espero que no

horn *(car)* la bocina *[botheena]*

horrible horrible *[orreeblay]*

hors d'oeuvre entremeses

horse un caballo *[kabayo]*

horse riding la equitación *[ekeetath-yon]*

hose *(for car radiator)* un tubo flexible *[toobo flexeeblay]*

hospital el hospital *[ospeetal]*

hospitality la hospitalidad *[ospeetaleeda]*; **thank you for your hospitality** gracias por su hospitalidad

hostel *(youth etc)* el albergue *[albairgay]*

hot caliente *[kal-yentay]*; *(curry etc)* picante; **I'm hot** tengo calor; **something hot to eat** algo caliente para comer; **it's so hot today** hoy hace tanto calor *[athay]*

hotdog un perro caliente *[kal-yentay]*

hotel un hotel *[otel]*; **at my hotel** en mi hotel

hotel clerk el recepcionista del hotel *[rethepth-yoneesta]*

hotplate *(on cooker)* una placa

hot-water bottle una bolsa de agua caliente *[agwa kal-yentay]*

hour una hora *[ora]*; **on the hour** a la hora

house una casa

housewife una ama de casa

how como; **how many?** ¿cuántos? *[kwantos]*; **how much?** ¿cuánto? *[kwanto]*; **how often?** ¿cada cuánto tiempo? *[t-yempo]*; **how are you?** ¿cómo está?; **how do you do?** ¡mucho gusto!; **how about a beer?** ¿nos tomamos una cerveza? *[thairbay-tha]*; **how nice!** ¡qué bonito!; **would you show me how to?** ¿me enseña cómo hacerlo? *[may ensayn-ya komo athairlo]*

humid húmedo *[oomedo]*

humidity la humedad *[oomeda]*

humo(u)r: where's your sense of humo(u)r? ¿no tienes sentido del humor? *[... t-yenays ... oomor]*

hundredweight *see page 118*

hungry: I'm hungry tengo hambre *[ambray]*; **I'm not hungry** no tengo hambre

hurry: I'm in a hurry tengo prisa; **hurry up!** ¡dese prisa! *[day-say]*; **there's no hurry** no hay prisa *[no eye]*
hurt: it hurts me me duele *[may dway-lay]*; **my back hurts me** me duele la espalda
husband: my husband mi marido
hydrofoil un hidrofoil *[eedro—]*

I

I yo; **I am English** soy inglés; **I live in Manchester** vivo en Manchester *[beebo ...] see page 105*
ice el hielo *[yay-lo]*; **with ice** con hielo
ice-cream un helado *[elado]*
ice-cream cone un helado de cucurucho *[kookooroocho]*
iced coffee un café helado *[kafay elado]*
ice lolly un polo
idea una idea *[eeday-a]*; **good idea!** ¡buena idea! *[bwena]*
ideal ideal *[eeday-al]*
identity papers los documentos de identidad *[dokoomentos day eedentee-da]*
idiot un/una idiota *[eed-yota]*
idyllic idílico
if si *[see]*; **if you could** si puede *[pway-day]*; **if not** si no
ignition el encendido *[enthendeedo]*
ill enfermo *[enfairmo]*; **I feel ill** me encuentro mal *[may enkwentro]*
illegal ilegal *[ee-laygal]*
illegible ilegible *[eele-неeblay]*
illness una enfermedad *[enfairmayda]*
imitation (*leather etc*) de imitación *[day eemeetath-yon]*
immediately ahora mismo *[a-ora meezmo]*
immigration la inmigración *[eemee-grath-yon]*
import importar
important importante; **it's very important** es muy importante *[es mwee]*; **it's not important** no tiene importancia *[no t-yenay eemportanth-ya]*
impossible imposible *[eemposseeblay]*
impressive impresionante *[eempress-*

yonantay]
improve: it's improving está mejorando *[me-ноrando]*; **I want to improve my Spanish** quiero perfeccionar mi español *[k-yairo pairfekth-yonar mee espan-yol]*
in: in my room en mi habitación *[abee-tath-yon]*; **in London** en Londres; **in one hour's time** dentro de una hora *[ora]*; **in August** en agosto; **in English** en inglés; **in Spanish** en español; **is he in?** ¿está?
inch una pulgada *[poolgada] see page 117*
include incluir *[een-klweer]*; **does that include meals?** ¿eso incluye las comidas? *[eenklooyay]*; **is that included in the price?** ¿está eso incluido en el precio? *[eenklweedo]*
inclusive incluido *[eenklweedo]*
incompetent incompetente
inconsiderate desconsiderado
inconvenient inoportuno *[—oono]*
increase un aumento *[owmento]*
incredible increíble *[eenkray-eeblay]*
indecent indecente *[eendethentay]*
independent independiente *[—yentay]*
India India *[eend-ya]*
Indian indio/a *[eend-yo]*
indicator el indicador
indigestion una indigestión *[eendee-неst-yon]*
indoor pool una piscina cubierta *[pees-theena koob-yairta]*
indoors dentro
industry la industria *[eendoostr-ya]*
inefficient ineficiente *[eenefeeth-yentay]*
infection una infección *[eenfekth-yon]*
infectious infeccioso *[eenfekth-yoso]*

inflammation una inflamación *[—ath-yon]*
inflation la inflación *[eenflath-yon]*
informal *(function)* informal
information la información *[—ath-yon]*
information desk *(at airport etc)* información *[—ath-yon]*
information office la oficina de información *[ofeetheena day eenformath-yon]*
injection una inyección *[een-yekth-yon]*
injured herido *[ereedo]*; **she's been injured** está herida
injury una herida *[ereeda]*
in-law: my in-laws mi familia política
innocent inocente *[eenothentay]*
inquisitive curioso *[koor-yoso]*
insect un insecto
insect bite una picadura de insecto
insecticide un insecticida *[—theeda]*
insect repellent una loción contra los insectos *[loth-yon]*
inside: inside the tent dentro de la tienda; **let's sit inside** vamos a sentarnos adentro *[bamos]*
insincere poco sincero *[seenthairo]*
insist: I insist insisto
insomnia insomnio *[eensomn-yo]*
instant coffee un café instantáneo *[kafay eenstantanay-o]*
instead en cambio; **I'll have that one instead** deme ese otro *[daymay]*; **instead of ...** en lugar de ... *[en loogar day]*
insulating tape una cinta aislante *[theenta eye-slantay]*
insulin la insulina *[eensooleena]*
insult un insulto *[eensoolto]*
insurance el seguro *[segooro]*; **write your insurance company here** ponga el nombre de su compañía de seguros aquí *[... kompanyee-a ...]*
insurance policy una póliza de seguros *[poleetha]*
intellectual intelectual *[—wal]*
intelligent inteligente *[—Hentay]*
intentional: it wasn't intentional ha sido sin querer *[seen kairair]*
interest: places of interest los lugares de interés *[loogarays]*
interested: I'm very interested in ... estoy muy interesado en ... *[... mwee ...]*
interesting interesante; **that's very in-**

teresting eso es muy interesante *[... mwee ...]*
international internacional *[eentairnath-yonal]*
interpret: would you interpret? ¿puede traducir? *[pway-day tradootheer]*
interpreter un/a intérprete *[eentairpre-tay]*
intersection un cruce *[kroothay]*
interval *(in play etc)* un descanso
into en; **I'm not into that** no me gusta eso *[no may goosta]*
introduce: may I introduce ...? le presento a ...
introvert un introvertido *[eentrobair-teedo]*
invalid un inválido *[eembaleedo]*
invalid chair una silla de inválido *[see-ya day]*
invitation una invitación *[eembeetath-yon]*; **thank you for the invitation** gracias por la invitación
invite invitar *[eembeetar]*; **can I invite you out?** ¿te gustaría salir conmigo? *[tay goostaree-a]*
involved: I don't want to get involved in it no quiero tener nada que ver con eso *[no k-yairo tenair nada kay bair]*
iodine el yodo
Ireland Irlanda *[eerlanda]*
Irish irlandés *[eerlandays]*
Irishman un irlandés *[eerlandays]*
Irishwoman una irlandesa *[eerlandaysa]*
iron *(for clothes)* una plancha; **can you iron these for me?** ¿puede planchármelos? *[pway-day plancharmay-los]*
ironmonger una ferretería
is es, está *see pages 110, 115*
island una isla *[eesla]*; **on the island** en la isla
isolated aislado *[eye-slado]*
it lo; **is it ...?** ¿es ...?, ¿está ...?; **where is it?** ¿dónde está?; **it's her** es ella *[eya]*; **it's only me** soy yo; **it was ...** era ...; **that's just it!** ¡eso es!; **that's it** *(that's right)* está bien *[b-yen] see page 105*
Italy Italia
Italian italiano
itch: it itches me pica *[may]*
itinerary el itinerario

J

jack (*for car*) el gato
jacket una chaqueta [*chakay-ta*]
jacuzzi un jacuzzi [*Hakoothee*]
jam mermelada; **traffic jam** un atasco; **I
  jammed on the brakes** frené de repente
  [*fraynay day raypentay*]
January enero
jaundice ictericia [*eektaireeth-ya*]
jaw la mandíbula [*mandeeboola*]
jazz el jazz
jazz club un club de jazz [*kloob*]
jealous celoso [*theloso*]; **he's jealous** está
  celoso
jeans unos vaqueros [*bakairos*]
jellyfish una medusa [*medoosa*]
jet-setter un miembro de la jet-set [*m-
  yembro*]
jetty el muelle [*mwe-yay*]
Jew un judío [*Hoodee-o*]
jewel(le)ry las joyas [*Hoyas*]
Jewish judío [*Hoodee-o*]
jiffy: **just a jiffy!** ¡un momento!
job un trabajo [*traba-Ho*]; **just the job!**
  ¡estupendo! [*estoopendo*]; **it's a good
  job you told me!** ¡menos mal que me lo
  dijo! [*may lo dee-Ho*]
jog: **I'm going for a jog** voy a hacer
  footing [*athair footin*]
jogging el footing
join (*club etc*) hacerse socio [*athair-say
  soth-yo*]; **I'd like to join** me gustaría
  hacerme socio [*athair-may soth-yo*]; **can
  I join you?** (*at table*) ¿puedo sentarme?
  [*pway-do*]; (*go with you*) ¿puedo ir con
  usted(es)? [*oostay(days)*]; **do you want
  to join us?** ¿quiere venir con nosotros?

[*k-yairay beneer*]
joint (*in bone*) una articulación [*artee-
  koolath-yon*]; (*to smoke*) un porro
joke un chiste [*cheestay*]; **you've got to
  be joking!** ¿lo dices en serio? [*lo deethays
  en sair-yo*]; **it's no joke** no es cosa de risa
jolly: **it was jolly good** era estupendo
  [*estoopendo*]; **jolly good!** ¡estupendo!
journey un viaje [*b-ya-Hay*]; **have a good
  journey!** ¡buen viaje! [*bwen b-ya-Hay*];
  safe journey! ¡buen viaje!
jug una jarra [*Harra*]; **a jug of water** una
  jarra de agua [*agwa*]
July julio [*Hool-yo*]
jump: **you made me jump** me ha dado un
  susto [*may a dado oon soosto*]; **jump in!**
  (*to car*) ¡sube! [*soobay*]
jumper un jersey [*Hair-say*]
jump leads unas pinzas (para la batería)
  [*peenthas*]
junction un cruce [*kroothay*]
June junio [*Hoon-yo*]
junior: **Mr Jones junior** Sr. Jones, hijo
  [*ee-Ho*]
junk baratijas [*baratee-Has*]
just: **just the one** lo justo [*Hoos-to*]; **just
  me** sólo yo; **just for me** sólo para mí; **just
  a little** sólo un poquito [*pokeeto*]; **just
  here** aquí mismo [*akee meezmo*]; **not
  just now** ahora no [*a-ora no*]; **he was
  here just now** estaba aquí hace un momento [*... akee athay ...*]; **that's just
  right** así está bien [*asee ... b-yen*]; **it's
  just as good** es igual de bueno [*es eegwal
  day bweno*]; **that's just as well** menos
  mal

K

kagul un chubasquero [*choobaskairo*]
keen: I'm not keen no tengo ganas
keep: can I keep it? ¿puedo quedarme con ello? [*pway-do kaydar-may*]; **you can keep it** puede quedárselo [*pway-day kaydarsay-lo*]; **keep the change** quédese con el cambio [*kaydaysay*]; **will it keep?** (*food*) ¿no se pondrá malo?; **it's keeping me awake** no me deja dormir [*no may day-нa*]; **it keeps on breaking** se rompe continuamente [*say rompay*]; **I can't keep anything down** (*food*) todo lo devuelvo [*debwelbo*]
kerb el bordillo [*bordee-yo*]
ketchup el ketchup
key la llave [*yabay*]
kid: the kids los niños [*neen-yos*]; **I'm not kidding** no es broma
kidneys los riñones [*reen-yones*]
kill matar
kilo un kilo *see page 118*
kilometre, kilometer un kilómetro *see page 117*
kind: that's very kind es muy amable [*mwee amablay*]; **this kind of ...** esta clase de ... [*klassay*]

kiosk un quiosco [*k-yosko*]
kiss un beso
kitchen la cocina [*kotheena*]
kitchenette una cocina pequeña
Kleenex (*tm*) un kleenex
knackered rendido
knee la rodilla [*rodee-ya*]
knickers unas bragas
knife un cuchillo [*koochee-yo*]
knitting el punto
knitting needles unas agujas de punto [*agoo-нas*]
knock: there's a knocking noise from the engine suena un golpeteo en el motor [*swayna oon golpetay-o*]; **he's had a knock on the head** se ha dado un golpe en la cabeza [*say a dado oon golpay*]; **he's been knocked over** le han atropellado [*atropey-ado*]
knot (*in rope*) un nudo [*noodo*]
know (*somebody*) conocer [*konothair*]; (*something*) saber [*sabair*]; **I don't know** no sé [*no say*]; **do you know a good restaurant?** ¿conoce un buen restaurante? [*konothay*]; **who knows?** ¿quién sabe? [*k-yen sabay*]

L

label la etiqueta [*eteekay-ta*]
laces los cordones
lacquer la laca
ladies' (room) los aseos de señoras [*assayos day sen-yoras*]
lady una señora [*sen-yora*]; **ladies and gentlemen!** ¡señoras y señores!
lager una cerveza [*thairbay-tha*]; **lager**

and lime una cerveza con lima
lake el lago
lamb cordero [*kordairo*]
lamp una lámpara
lamppost una farola
lampshade una pantalla [*panta-ya*]
land (*not sea*) tierra firme [*t-yairra*]; **when does the plane land?** ¿a qué hora aterri-

za el avión? *[a kay ora atairreetha el ab-yon]*

landscape el paisaje *[py-sa-нay]*

lane (*car*) el carril; (*narrow road*) una callejuela *[kayay-нwayla]*

language idioma *[eed-yoma]*

language course (*for Spanish*) un curso de español *[espan-yol]*

large grande

laryngitis laringitis *[lareen-нeetees]*

last último *[oolteemo]*; **last year** el año pasado *[an-yo]*; **last Wednesday** el miércoles pasado *[m-yairkolays]*; **last night** anoche *[anotchay]*; **when is the last bus?** ¿a qué hora sale el último autobús? *[oolteemo owtoboos]*; **one last drink** la última copa; **when were you last in London?** ¿cuándo fue la última vez que estuvo en Londres? *[kwando fway la oolteema beth]*; **at last!** ¡por fin!; **how long does it last?** (*film etc*) ¿cuánto dura? *[kwanto doora]*; **last name** el apellido *[a-pe-yeedo]*

late: sorry I'm late perdone que haya llegado tarde *[pairdonay kay aya yaygado tarday]*; **don't be late** no llegue tarde *[no yaygay]*; **the bus was late** el autobús llegó tarde *[owtoboos yaygo]*; **we'll be back late** regresaremos tarde; **it's getting late** se hace tarde *[say athay]*; **is it that late!** ¡es ésa la hora!; **it's too late now** es demasiado tarde ahora; **I'm a late riser** me levanto tarde *[may lebanto]*

lately últimamente *[oolteemamentay]*

later más tarde; **later on** más tarde; **I'll come back later** volveré más tarde *[bolbair-ay]*; **see you later** hasta luego *[asta lway-go]*; **no later than Tuesday** para el martes a más tardar

latest: the latest news las últimas noticias *[oolteemas noteeth-yas]*; **at the latest** lo más tarde

laugh la risa; **don't laugh** ne se ría *[no say ree-a]*; **it's no laughing matter** no tiene ninguna gracia *[t-yenay neen-goona grath-ya]*

launderette, laundromat una lavandería automática *[labandairee-a owtomateeka]*

laundry (*clothes*) la ropa sucia *[sooth-ya]*; (*place*) la lavandería *[labandairee-a]*; **could you get the laundry done?** ¿po-

drían lavarme la ropa? *[podree-an labarmay]*

lavatory el lavabo *[lababo]*

law la ley *[lay-ee]*; **against the law** contra la ley

lawn el césped *[thesped]*

lawyer un abogado

laxative un laxante

lay-by un arcén *[arthen]*

laze around: I just want to laze around sólo quiero descansar *[k-yairo]*

lazy perezoso *[pairethoso]*; **don't be lazy** no sea perezoso *[no say-a]*; **a nice lazy holiday** unas vacaciones relajadas *[bakath-yonays rela-нadas]*

lead (*elec*) el cable *[kablay]*; **where does this road lead?** ¿adónde va esta carretera? *[… ba …]*

leaf una hoja *[o-нa]*

leaflet un folleto *[fo-yayto]*; **do you have any leaflets on …?** ¿tiene algún folleto sobre …? *[t-yenay]*

leak una gotera; (*gas*) fuga *[fooga]*; **the roof leaks** el tejado gotea *[gotay-a]*

learn: I want to learn … quiero aprender … *[k-yairo aprendair]*

learner: I'm just a learner estoy aprendiendo

lease arrendar

least: not in the least de ninguna manera *[day neengoona manaira]*; **at least 50** por lo menos cincuenta

leather (*fine*) piel *[p-yel]*; (*heavy*) cuero *[kwairo]*

leave: when does the bus leave? ¿a qué hora sale el autobús? *[a kay ora salay el owtoboos]*; **I leave tomorrow** me marcho mañana; **he left this morning** se marchó esta mañana; **may I leave this here?** ¿puedo dejar esto aquí? *[pway-do de-нar]*; **I left my bag in the bar** olvidé el bolso en el bar *[olbeeday]*; **she left her bag here** olvidó su bolso aquí *[olbeedo]*; **leave the window open please** deje la ventana abierta, por favor *[day-нay la bentana ab-yairta]*; **there's not much left** no queda mucho *[kayda]*; **I've hardly any money left** casi no me queda dinero; **I'll leave it up to you** le dejo a usted la decisión *[lay day-нo a oostay la dethees-yon]*

lecher un obseso sexual *[sekswal]*

left izquierdo *[eethk-yairdo]*; **on the left** a

la izquierda
left-handed zurdo *[thoordo]*
lefthand drive con el volante a la izquierda *[bolantay a la eethk-yairda]*
left luggage (*office*) la consigna de equipaje *[konseegna day ekeepa-нay]*
leg la pierna *[p-yairna]*
legal legal *[lay-gal]*
legal aid asistencia legal *[aseestenth-ya]*
lemon un limón
lemonade una limonada
lemon tea un té con limón *[tay]*
lend: would you lend me your ...? ¿podría prestarme su ...? *[podree-a]*
lens (*camera*) el objetivo *[ob-нeteebo]*; (*contact*) la lentilla *[lentee-ya]*
Lent la Cuaresma *[kwarezma]*
lesbian una lesbiana
less: less than an hour menos de una hora *[maynos]*; **less than that** menos que eso; **less hot** menos caliente
lesson una lección *[lekth-yon]*; **do you give lessons?** ¿da clases?
let: would you let me use it? ¿me dejaría usarlo? *[may day-нaree-a oosarlo]*; **will you let me know?** ¿me lo dirá? *[may lo deera]*; **I'll let you know** se lo diré *[say lo deeray]*; **let me try** déjeme probar *[day-нaymay]*; **let me go!** ¡suélteme! *[sweltay-may]*; **let's leave now** ¡vámonos! *[bamonos]*; **let's stay a bit longer** ¿por qué no nos quedamos otro rato? *[por kay ... kay-damos ...]*; **will you let me off at ...?** ¿me avisa cuando lleguemos a ...? *[may abeesa kwando yay-gay mos]*; **room to let** una habitación para alquilar *[abeetath-yon para alkeelar]*
letter una carta; **are there any letters for me?** ¿hay cartas para mí? *[eye ... mee]*
letterbox un buzón *[boothon]*
lettuce una lechuga *[lechooga]*
level crossing un paso a nivel *[neebel]*
lever la palanca
liable (*responsible*) responsable *[—ablay]*
liberated: a liberated woman una mujer liberada *[moo-hair]*
library una biblioteca *[beebl-yotayka]*
licence, license el permiso *[pairmeeso]*
license plate la placa de matrícula *[matreekoola]*
lid la tapa
lido una piscina al aire libre *[peestheena*

al *eye-ray leebray]*
lie (*untruth*) una mentira *[men-teera]*; **can she lie down for a while?** ¿se podría acostar un rato?; **I want to go and lie down** quiero ir a echarme *[k-yairo ... aycharmay]*
lie-in: I'm going to have a lie-in tomorrow voy a levantarme tarde mañana *[boy a lebantar-may]*
life la vida *[beeda]*; **that's life** así es la vida; **not on your life!** ¡jamás! *[нamas]*
lifebelt un salvavidas *[salbabeedas]*
lifeboat (*on shore*) una lancha salvavidas *[salbabeedas]*; (*on boat*) un bote salvavidas
lifeguard el bañero *[ban-yay-ro]*
life insurance el seguro de vida *[segooro day beeda]*
life jacket el chaleco salvavidas *[salbabeedas]*
lift (*in hotel*) el ascensor *[asthensor]*; **could you give me a lift?** ¿podría llevarme en su coche? *[podree-a yaybarmay]*; **do you want a lift?** ¿quiere que le lleve? *[k-yairay kay lay yaybay]*; **thanks for the lift** gracias por llevarme *[yaybarmay]*; **I got a lift** alguien me llevó *[alg-yen may yaybo]*
light la luz *[looth]*; (*not heavy*) ligero *[lee-нairo]*; **the light was on** la luz estaba encendida *[enthendeeda]*; **do you have a light?** ¿tiene fuego? *[t-yenay fwaygo]*; **a light meal** una comida ligera; **light blue** azul claro *[athool]*
light bulb una bombilla *[bombeeya]*
lighter (*cigarette*) un encendedor *[enthendedor]*
lighthouse el faro
light meter el fotómetro
lightning el relámpago
like: I'd like a ... quisiera un ... *[keesyaira]*; **I'd like to ...** quisiera ...; **would you like ...?** ¿quiere ...? *[k-yairay]*; **would you like to come too?** ¿quiere venir también?; **I like it** me gusta *[may goosta]*; **I like you** me gustas; **I don't like it** no me gusta; **he doesn't like it** no le gusta (a él); **do you like ...?** ¿le gusta ...?; **I like swimming** me gusta la natación; **OK, if you like** bueno, si quiere *[see k-yairay]*; **what's it like?** ¿cómo es?; **do it like this** hágalo así *[agalo asee]*; **one like that** uno así

lilo (*tm*) un colchón inflable *[inflablay]*
lime cordial un zumo de lima *[thoomo]*
lime juice un zumo de lima *[thoomo]*
line (*on paper, road*) la línea *[leenay-a]*; (*of people*) la cola; **would you give me a line?** (*tel*) ¿puede darme una línea? *[pway-day]*
linen (*for beds*) las sábanas
linguist un lingüista; **I'm no linguist** no se me dan los idiomas *[eed-yomas]*
lining (*clothes*) el forro
lip el labio *[lab-yo]*
lip brush pincel de labios *[peenthel day lab-yos]*
lip gloss el brillo de labios *[bree-yo day lab-yos]*
lip pencil un lápiz perfilador de labios *[lapeeth]*
lip salve una crema de labios
lipstick un lápiz de labios *[lapeeth]*
liqueur un licor
liquor una bebida alcohólica *[alk-oleeka]*
liquor store una tienda de vinos *[t-yenda day beenos]*
list una lista
listen: I'd like to listen to ... me gustaría escuchar a ... *[may goostaree-a eskoochar]*; **listen!** ¡escuche! *[eskoochay]*
liter, litre un litro *see page 118*
litter la basura *[basoora]*
little pequeño *[paykayn-yo]*; **just a little, thanks** sólo un poco, por favor; **just a very little** sólo un poquito *[pokeeto]*; **a little cream** un poco de nata; **a little more** un poco más; **a little better** un poco mejor *[me-нor]*; **that's too little** (*not enough*) es demasiado poco
live vivir *[beebeer]*; **I live in Manchester/Texas** vivo en Manchester/ Tejas *[tay-нas]*; **where do you live?** ¿dónde vive? *[donday beebay]*; **where does he live?** ¿dónde vive (él)?; **we live together** vivimos juntos *[нoontos]*
lively (*town, person etc*) alegre
liver el hígado *[eegado]*
lizard un lagarto; (*small*) una lagartija *[la-gartee-нa]*
loaf un pan
lobby (*in hotel*) el vestíbulo *[besteeboolo]*
lobster una langosta
local: a local wine un vino de la región *[beeno day la reн-yon]*; **a local newspaper** un periódico local; **a local**

restaurant un restaurante local *[restowrantay]*
lock la cerradura *[thairradoora]*; **it's locked** está cerrado con llave *[thairrado kon yabay]*; **I've locked myself out of my room** olvidé la llave en la habitación *[olbeeday la yabay en la abeetath-yon]*
locker (*for luggage etc*) una consigna automática *[konseegna]*
log: I slept like a log dormí como un lirón
lollipop un chupa-chups (*tm*) *[choopa-choops]*; (*iced*) un polo
London Londres *[londrays]*
lonely solitario; **are you lonely?** ¿se siente solo? *[say s-yentay]*
long largo; **how long does it take?** ¿cuánto tiempo tarda? *[kwanto t-yempo]*; **is it a long way** ¿queda lejos? *[kayda lay-нos]*; **a long time** mucho tiempo; **I won't be long** no tardaré *[tardaray]*; **don't be long** no tarde; **that was long ago** eso fue hace mucho tiempo *[fway athay]*; **I'd like to stay longer** me gustaría quedarme más tiempo *[may goostaree-a kaydarmay]*; **long time no see!** ¡cuánto tiempo sin verte! *[kwanto t-yempo seen bairtay]*; **so long!** ¡hasta luego! *[asta lwaygo]*
long distance call una conferencia *[konfairenth-ya]*
long drink un refresco
loo: where's the loo? ¿dónde está el baño?; **I want to go to the loo** quiero ir al baño *[k-yairo]*
look: that looks good eso parece bien *[par-ethay b-yen]*; **you look tired** parece cansado; **I'm just looking, thanks** estoy mirando, gracias; **you don't look it** (*your age*) no lo parece; **look at him** mírelo *[meeraylo]*; **I'm looking for ...** estoy buscando ...; **look out!** ¡cuidado! *[kwee-dado]*; **can I have a look?** ¿puedo ver? *[pway-do bair]*; **can I have a look around?** ¿puedo echar una ojeada? *[pway-do aychar oona o-нayada]*
loose (*button, handle etc*) suelto *[swelto]*
loose change cambio
lorry un camión *[kam-yon]*
lorry driver un camionero *[kam-yonai-ro]*
lose perder *[pairdair]*; **I've lost my ...** he perdido mi ... *[ay pairdeedo mee]*; **I'm lost** estoy perdido

lost property office, lost and found la oficina de objetos perdidos *[ofeetheena day ob-нaytos pairdeedos]*

lot: a lot, lots mucho, muchos; **not a lot** no mucho; **a lot of money** mucho dinero; **a lot of women** muchas mujeres *[moo-нairays]*; **a lot cooler** mucho más fresco; **I like it a lot** me gusta mucho *[may goosta]*; **is it a lot further?** ¿falta mucho para llegar? *[yaygar]*; **I'll take the (whole) lot** me lo llevo todo *[may lo yaybo]*

lotion una loción *[loth-yon]*

loud fuerte *[fwairtay]*; **the music is rather loud** la música está bastante fuerte

lounge (*in hotel*) el salón; (*airport*) la sala de espera; (*in chalet*) la sala

lousy pésimo

love: I love you te quiero *[tay k-yairo]*; **he's fallen in love** se ha enamorado; **I love Spain** me encanta España *[may]*; **let's make love** hagamos el amor *[agamos]*

lovely encantador

low bajo *[ba-нo]*

low beam las luces cortas *[loothays]*

LP un LP *[elay-pay]*

luck la suerte *[swairtay]*; **hard luck!** ¡mala suerte!; **good luck!** ¡buena suerte! *[bwena]*; **just my luck!** ¡qué mala suerte!; **it was pure luck** ¡fue pura suerte! *[fway poora]*

lucky: that's lucky! ¡qué suerte! *[kay swairtay]*

lucky charm un amuleto (de buena suerte)

luggage el equipaje *[ekeepa-нay]*

lumbago lumbago *[loomba-go]*

lump (*on skin*) una hinchazón *[eenchathon]*

lunch el almuerzo *[almwairtho]*

lungs los pulmones *[poolmonays]*

Luxembourg Luxemburgo

luxurious de lujo *[loo-нo]*

luxury el lujo *[loo-нo]*

M

macho varonil *[baroneel]*

mad loco

madam señora *[sen-yora]*

magazine una revista *[rebeesta]*

magnificent magnífico

maid (*in hotel*) una camarera *[—raira]*

maiden name el nombre de soltera

mail: is there any mail for me? ¿hay correspondencia para mí? *[eye —denth-ya]*

mailbox un buzón *[boothon]*

main principal *[preetheepal]*; **where's the main post office?** ¿dónde está la oficina principal de correos? *[korray-os]*

main road la calle principal *[ka-yay preentheepal]*; (*in the country*) la carretera principal *[—taira]*

male chauvinist pig un machista

make hacer *[athair]*; **do you make them yourself?** ¿los hace usted mismo? *[athay oostay meezmo]*; **it's very well made** está muy bien hecho *[mwee b-yen aycho]*; **what does that make altogether?** ¿cuánto es todo? *[kwanto]*; **I make it only 520 pesetas** creo que son sólo 520 pesetas *[krayo kay]*

make up el maquillaje *[makeeya-нay]*

make-up remover la crema desmaquilladora *[dezmakee-yadora]*

man un hombre *[ombray]*

manager el gerente *[нairentay]*; **may I see the manager?** quiero ver al gerente *[k-yairo bair]*

manageress la gerente *[нairentay]*

manicure una manicura *[maneekoora]*

many muchos *[moochos]*

map: a map of ... un mapa de ...; **it's not on this map** no está en este mapa

marble el mármol

March marzo *[martho]*

margarine la margarina

marijuana la marihuana [*maree-wana*]

mark: there's a mark on it tiene un defecto [*t-yenay*]; **could you mark it on the map for me?** ¿podría marcármelo en el mapa? [*podree-a markarmaylo*]

market un mercado [*mairkado*]

marmalade una mermelada de naranja [*mairmelada day naran-нa*]

married: are you married? ¿está casado?; **I'm married** estoy casado

mascara un rímel

mask una máscara; (*for diving*) una mascarilla [*—ree-ya*]

mass: I'd like to go to mass quisiera ir a misa [*kees-yaira eer a meesa*]

massage un masaje [*masa-нay*]

mast el mástil

masterpiece una obra maestra [*my-estra*]

match (*sport*) un partido [*parteedo*]

matches unas cerillas [*thairee-yas*]

material (*cloth*) un tejido [*te-нeedo*]

matter: it doesn't matter no importa; **what's the matter?** ¿qué pasa? [*kay*]

mattress un colchón

maximum máximo

May mayo [*ma-yo*]

may: may I have another bottle? ¿me trae otra botella? [*may tra-ay*]; **may I?** ¿puedo? [*pway-do*]

maybe tal vez [*beth*]; **maybe not** tal vez no

mayonnaise la mayonesa

me: come with me venga conmigo [*konmeego*]; **it's for me** es para mí [*mee*]; **it's me** soy yo; **me too** yo también [*tamb-yen*]; *see page 105*

meal: that was an excellent meal la comida estaba riquísima [*komeeda ... reekeeseema*]; **does that include meals?** ¿incluye las comidas? [*eenklooyay*]

mean: what does this word mean? ¿qué significa esta palabra?; **what does he mean?** ¿qué quiere decir? [*kay k-yairay detheer*]

measles el sarampión [*—yon*]; **German measles** la rubéola [*roobay-ola*]

measurements las medidas

meat la carne

mechanic: do you have a mechanic here? ¿hay algún mecánico aquí? [*akee*]

medicine la medicina [*medeetheena*]

medieval medieval [*maid-yaybal*]

Mediterranean el Mediterráneo [*—anay-o*]

medium medio [*mayd-yo*]

medium-dry semi-seco

medium-rare (*steak*) un poco hecho [*ay-cho*]

medium-sized de tamaño medio [*taman-yo*]

medium sweet semi-dulce [*doolthay*]

meet: pleased to meet you mucho gusto [*moocho goosto*]; **where shall we meet?** ¿dónde nos vemos? [*baymos*]; **let's meet up again** ¿podemos vernos otra vez? [*bairnos otra beth*]

meeting (*business etc*) una reunión [*ray-oon-yon*]

meeting place un lugar de reunión [*loogar*]

melon un melón

member un socio [*soth-yo*]; **I'd like to become a member** me gustaría hacerme socio [*goostaree-a athairmay*]

mend: can you mend this? ¿puede arreglarme esto? [*pway-day*]

men's room los servicios [*sairbeeth-yos*]

mention: don't mention it de nada

menu el menú [*menoo*]

mess un lío [*lee-o*]

message: are there any messages for me? ¿hay algún recado para mí? [*eye*]; **I'd like to leave a message for ...** quisiera dejar un recado para ... [*kees-yaira day-нar*]

metal el metal

metre, meter un metro *see page 117*

midday: at midday a mediodía [*mayd-yodee-a*]

middle: in the middle en el medio [*mayd-yo*]; **in the middle of the road** en medio de la calle [*ka-yay*]; **in the middle ages** en la edad media

middle-aged de mediana edad [*mayd-yana ayda*]

midnight: at midnight a medianoche [*mayd-yanochay*]

might: I might want to stay another 3 days quizás decida quedarme otros tres días [*keethas day-theeda kaydarmay*]; **you might have warned me!** ¡podría haberme avisado! [*podree-a abairmay*]; **I might** es posible [*poseeblay*]

migraine una jaqueca [*нakay-ka*]

mild suave *[swabay]*; (*weather*) templado
mile una milla *[mee-ya]*; **that's miles away!** eso queda muÿ lejos *[kay-da mwee lay-HOS] see page 117*
military militar
milk la leche *[lechay]*
milkshake un batido
millimetre, millimeter un milímetro
minced meat la carne picada
mind: I don't mind no me importa; (*either will do etc*) me es igual *[eeg-wal]*; **would you mind if I ...?** ¿le importa si ...?; **never mind!** ¡qué más da! *[kay]*; **I've changed my mind** he cambiado de idea *[ay ... eeday-a]*
mine: it's mine es mío *see page 107*
mineral water agua mineral *[ag-wa]*
minimum mínimo
mint (*sweet*) un caramelo de menta *[karamay-lo]*
minus menos *[maynos]*; **minus 3 degrees** tres grados bajo cero *[ba-HO thairo]*
minute un minuto; **in a minute** en seguida *[segeeda]*; **just a minute** un momento
mirror un espejo *[espay-HO]*
Miss Señorita *[sen-yoreeta]*
miss: I miss you te echo de menos *[tay aycho day maynos]*; **there is a ... missing** falta un ...; **we missed the bus** hemos perdido el autobús *[aymos ... owtoboos]*; **I'm going to miss the boat!** voy a perder el barco *[boy a pairdair]*
mist la niebla *[n-yaybla]*; (*sea*) la bruma *[brooma]*
mistake un error; **I think there's a mistake here** me parece que se ha equivocado aquí *[may pa-rethay say a ekeebokado akee]*
misunderstanding un malentendido
mixture una mezcla *[methkla]*
mix-up: there's been some sort of mix-up with ... ha habido una confusión con ... *[a abeedo oona konfoos-yon]*
modern moderno *[modairno]*; **a modern art gallery** una galería de arte moderno
moisturizer una crema hidratante *[eedratantay]*
moment un momento; **I won't be a moment** vuelvo enseguida *[bwelbo ensegeeda]*
monastery un monasterio
Monday lunes *[loonays]*

money el dinero *[deenairo]*; **I don't have any money** no tengo dinero; **do you take English/American money?** ¿acepta libras/dólares? *[athepta]*
month un mes *[mays]*
monument un monumento; (*statue*) una estatua *[estatoo-a]*
moon la luna *[loona]*
Moor un moro
moorings el amarradero *[—dairo]*
Moorish morisco *[moreesko]*
moped un ciclomotor *[theeklo—]*
more más; **may I have some more?** ¿me da un poco más?; **more water, please** más agua, por favor; **no more** basta, gracias; **more expensive** más caro; **more than 50/that** más de cincuenta/que eso; **a lot more** mucho más; **not any more** ya no más; **I don't stay there any more** ya no vivo allí *[a-yee]*
morning la mañana *[man-yana]*; **good morning** buenos días *[bwenos dee-as]*; **this morning** esta mañana; **in the morning** por la mañana
Moroccan marroquí *[marrokee]*
Morocco Marruecos *[marrwaykos]*
Moslem un musulmán *[moosoolman]*
mosque una mezquita *[methkeeta]*
mosquito un mosquito
most: I like this one most éste es el que más me gusta; **most of the time** la mayor parte del tiempo *[ma-yor partay]*; **most of the hotels** la mayoría de los hoteles *[ma-yoree-a]*
mother: my mother mi madre *[mee madray]*
motif (*in patterns*) el motivo
motor el motor
motorbike una moto
motorboat una motora
motorist un motorista
motorway una autopista *[owtopeesta]*
motor yacht un yate *[ya-tay]*
mountain una montaña *[montan-ya]*; **up in the mountains** en las montañas; **a mountain village** un pueblo de montaña *[pweblo]*
mouse un ratón
moustache un bigote *[beegotay]*
mouth la boca
move: he's moved to another hotel se fue a otro hotel *[say fway]*; **could you move your car?** ¿podría cambiar de sitio

su coche? *[podree-a kamb-yar day seet-yo]*
movie una película; **let's go to the movies** vamos al cine *[bamos al theenay]*
movie camera una cámara de cine *[theenay]*
movie theater un cine *[theenay]*
moving: a very moving tune una melodía muy conmovedora *[konmobaydora]*
Mr Señor *[sen-yor]*
Mrs Señora *[sen-yora]*
Ms Doña *[don-ya]*
much mucho *[moocho]*; **much better** mucho mejor; **much cooler** mucho más fresco; **not much** no mucho; **not so much** no tanto
mud el barro
muffler (*on car*) el silenciador *[seelenthyador]*
mug: I've been mugged me han asaltado *[may an]*

muggy húmedo *[oomaydo]*
mule una mula *[moola]*
mumps las paperas *[papairas]*
murals los murales *[mooral-ays]*
muscle un músculo *[mooskoolo]*
museum el museo *[moosay-o]*
mushrooms unos champiñones *[champeen-yonays]*
music la música *[mooseeka]*; **guitar music** la música de guitarras; **do you have the sheet music for ...?** ¿tiene la partitura de ...? *[t-yenay la partee-toora]*
musician un músico *[mooseeko]*
mussels unos mejillones *[me-нeeyonays]*
must: I must ... tengo que ... *[kay]*; **I mustn't drink ...** no debo beber *[daybo]*; **you mustn't forget** no se olvide *[no say olbeeday]*
mustache un bigote *[beegotay]*
mustard la mostaza *[mostatha]*
my mi *[mee] see page 103*
myself: I'll do it myself lo haré yo mismo *[aray yo meezmo]*

N

nail (*finger*) una uña *[oon-ya]*; (*wood*) un clavo *[klabo]*
nail clippers un cortauñas *[korta-oon-yas]*
nailfile una lima para las uñas *[oon-yas]*
nail polish esmalte para uñas *[ezmaltay para oon-yas]*
nail polish remover un quitaesmalte *[keeta-ezmaltay]*
nail scissors unas tijeritas de uñas *[tee-нaireetas day oon-yas]*
naked desnudo *[desnoodo]*
name el nombre *[nombray]*; **what's your name?** ¿cómo se llama usted? *[say yama oostay]*; **what's its name?** ¿cómo se llama?; **my name is ...** me llamo ... *[may yamo]*
nap: he's having a nap está echando una cabezada *[kabethada]*
napkin una servilleta *[sairbee-yayta]*

nappy un pañal *[pan-yal]*
narrow estrecho
nasty (*person, weather*) desagradable *[—ablay]*; (*taste, cut*) malo
national nacional *[nath-yonal]*
nationality la nacionalidad *[nath-yona-leeda]*
natural natural *[natooral]*
naturally naturalmente *[natooral—]*
nature la naturaleza *[natooralay-tha]*
naturist un/una naturista *[natooreesta]*
nausea una nausea *[nowsay-a]*
near: is it near here? ¿está cerca de aquí? *[thairka day akee]*; **near the window** cerca de la ventana; **do you go near ...?** ¿va a pasar usted cerca de ...? *[... oostay]*; **where is the nearest ...?** ¿dónde está el ... más cercano? *[thairkano]*
nearby por aquí cerca *[akee thairka]*
nearly casi *[ka-see]*

nearside (*wheel etc*) del lado de la cuneta [*koonayta*]

neat (*drink*) solo

necessary necesario [*nethesar-yo*]; **is it necessary to ...?** ¿es necesario ...?; **it's not necessary** no es necesario

neck el cuello [*kwe-yo*]

necklace un collar [*ko-yar*]

necktie una corbata

need: I need a ... necesito un ... [*netheseeto*]; **it needs more salt** le falta sal; **do I need to ...?** ¿necesito ...?; **there's no need** no hace falta [*no athay*]; **there's no need to shout!** ¡no hace falta que chille! [*chee-yay*]

needle una aguja [*agoo-нa*]

negative (*film*) el negativo [*—eebo*]

negotiation la negociación [*negoth-yathyon*]

neighbo(u)r un vecino [*betheeno*]

neighbo(u)rhood el vecindario [*betheendar-yo*]

neither: neither of us ninguno de nosotros; **neither one (of them)** ninguno (de ellos); **neither ... nor ...** ni ... ni ... [*nee*]; **neither do I** ni yo tampoco

nephew: my nephew mi sobrino

nervous nervioso [*nairb-yoso*]

net (*fishing, tennis*) la red; **£100 net** 100 libras

nettle una ortiga

neurotic neurótico [*nay-ooroteeko*]

neutral (*gear*) el punto muerto [*poonto mwairto*]

never nunca

new nuevo [*nway-bo*]; **could you put a new zip on?** ¿puede ponerme una crema-cremallera nueva? [*krayma-yaira*]

news (*TV etc*) las noticias [*noteeth-yas*]; **is there any news?** ¿hay noticias? [*eye*]

newspaper el periódico; **do you have any English newspapers?** ¿tiene usted algún periódico inglés? [*t-yenay oostay*]

newsstand una tienda de periódicos [*t-yenda*]

New Year el Año Nuevo [*an-yo nway-bo*]; **Happy New Year!** ¡Feliz Año Nuevo! [*feleeth*]

New Year's Eve Nochevieja [*notchay b-yay-нa*]

New York Nueva York [*nway-ba*]

New Zealand Nueva Zelanda [*nway-ba thelanda*]

New Zealander neozelandés [*nayo-thelandays*]

next próximo; **next to the post office** al lado de correos; **the one next to that** el de al lado de ése; **it's at the next corner** está en la siguiente esquina [*seeg-yentay eskeena*]; **next week/next Monday** la próxima semana/el próximo lunes

nextdoor al lado

next of kin el pariente más próximo [*par-yentay*]

nice (*town*) bonita; (*person*) simpático; (*meal*) buena; **that's very nice of you** es usted muy amable [*mwee amablay*]; **a nice cold drink** una bebida fría

nickname un apodo

niece: my niece mi sobrina

night noche [*notchay*]; **for one night** para una noche; **for three nights** para tres noches; **good night** buenas noches; **at night** por la noche

nightcap (*drink*) una copa

nightclub un cabaret

nightdress, nightie un camisón

night flight un vuelo nocturno [*bway-lo*]

night-life la vida nocturna [*beeda noctoorna*]

nightmare una pesadilla [*pesadee-ya*]

night porter el portero

nit (*bug*) un lindre [*leendray*]

no no; **I've no money** no tengo dinero; **there's no more** no hay más [*no eye mas*]; **no more than ...** no más de ...; **oh no!** (*upset*) ¡Dios mío! [*d-yos mee-o*]

nobody nadie [*nad-yay*]

noise un ruido [*rweedo*]

noisy ruidoso [*rweedoso*]; **it's too noisy** hay demasiado ruido

non-alcoholic sin alcohol [*alkol*]

none ninguno [*neengoono*]; **none of them** ninguno de ellos [*day eyos*]

nonsense tonterías

non-smoking no fumadores

non-stop (*drive etc*) sin parar

no-one nadie [*nad-yay*]

nor: nor do I yo tampoco

normal normal

north norte [*nortay*]; **to the north** al norte

northeast nordeste; **to the northeast** al nordeste

Northern Ireland Irlanda del Norte

northwest noroeste [*norwestay*]; **to the northwest** al noroeste

Norway Noruega *[norwayga]*
nose la nariz *[nareeth]*
nosebleed una hemorragia nasal *[emorraн-ya nassal]*
not no; **I don't smoke** no fumo; **he didn't say anything** no dijo nada *[no dee-нo]*; **it's not important** no importa; **not that one** ése no; **not for me** para mí no
note (*bank note*) un billete *[bee-yay-tay]*
notebook un cuaderno *[kwadairno]*
nothing nada
November noviembre *[nob-yembray]*
now ahora *[a-ora]*; **not now** ahora no
nowhere en ningún sitio *[en neengoon seet-yo]*
nudist nudista *[noo—]*

nudist beach una playa nudista *[ply-a]*
nuisance: he's being a nuisance nos está molestando
numb entumecido *[entoometheedo]*
number un número *[noo-]*; **what number?** ¿qué número?
number plate la placa de la matrícula *[matreekoola]*
nurse una enfermera *[enfairmaira]*
nursery (*at airport etc*) una guardería *[gwarderee-a]*
nursery slope la pista de principiantes *[day preentheep-yantes]*
nut una nuez *[nweth]*; (*for bolt*) una tuerca *[twairka]*
nutter: he's a nutter está como una cabra

O

oar un remo *[raymo]*
obligatory obligatorio
oblige: much obliged muchas gracias *[moochas grath-yas]*
obnoxious (*person*) desagradable *[—ablay]*
obvious: that's obvious eso es evidente *[ebeedentay]*
occasionally de vez en cuando *[day beth en kwando]*
o'clock *see page 116*
October octubre *[oktoobray]*
octopus un pulpo *[poolpo]*
odd (*number*) impar; (*strange*) raro *[ra-ro]*
odometer el cuentakilómetros *[kwenta—]*
of de *[day]*; **the name of the hotel** el nombre del hotel; **have one of mine** tome uno de los míos *[tomay]*
off: it just broke off se rompió; **20% off** un descuento del 20%; **the lights were off** las luces estaban apagadas *[loothays]*; **just off the main road** cerca de la carretera principal *[thairka]*
offend: don't be offended no se ofenda
office la oficina *[ofeetheena]*
officer (*said to policeman*) señor

official un oficial *[ofeeth-yal]*; **is that official?** ¿es oficial?
off-season fuera de temporada *[fwaira]*
off-side (*wheel etc*) del lado de la carretera
often a menudo *[a menoodo]*; **not often** pocas veces *[pokas bethays]*
oil (*for car, on salad*) el aceite *[athay-tay]*; **it's losing oil** se le va el aceite *[say lay ba]*; **will you change the oil?** ¿quiere cambiar el aceite? *[k-yairay]*; **the oil light's flashing** la luz del aceite está encendida *[looth ... enthendeeda]*
oil painting una pintura al óleo *[olay-o]*
oil pressure la presión del aceite *[press-yon day athay-tay]*
ointment una pomada
OK vale *[balay]*; **are you OK?** ¿está bien? *[b-yen]*; **that's OK thanks** está bien, gracias; **that's OK by me** estoy de acuerdo *[akwairdo]*
old viejo *[b-yay-нo]*; **how old are you?** ¿cuántos años tiene? *[kwantos an-yos t-yenay]*
old-age pensioner un pensionista *[pens-yoneesta]*
old-fashioned pasado de moda
old town la parte antigua (de la cuidad)

[anteegwa]
olive una aceituna *[athay-toona]*
olive oil el aceite de oliva *[athay-tay day oleeba]*
omelet(te) una tortilla *[torteeya]*
on en; **on the beach** en la playa *[ply-a]*; **on Friday** el viernes *[... b-yairnays]*; **on television** en la tele; **I don't have it on me** no lo llevo encima *[yaybo entheema]*; **this drink's on me** yo invito *[eembeeto]*; **a book on Madrid** un libro sobre Madrid; **the warning light comes on** la luz de peligro se enciende *[la looth ... enthyenday]*; **the light was on** la luz estaba encendida *[looth ... enthendeeda]*; **what's on in town?** ¿qué están poniendo en la ciudad? *[th-yooda]*; **it's just not on!** *(not acceptable)* ¡ni hablar!
once *(one time)* una vez *[beth]*; **at once** en seguida *[seg-eeda]*
one uno *[oono]*; **that one** ése; **the green one** el verde *[bairday]*; **the one with the black dress on** la del vestido negro; **the one in the blue shirt** el de la camisa azul
onion una cebolla *[theboy-a]*
only: only one sólo uno; **only once** sólo una vez *[beth]*; **it's only 9 o'clock** son sólo las 9; **I've only just arrived** acabo de llegar *[yaygar]*
open *(adjective)* abierto *[ab-yairto]*; **when do you open?** ¿a qué hora abre? *[a kay ora abray]*; **in the open** al aire libre *[eye-ray leebray]*; **it won't open** no se abre *[abray]*
opening times *(of bank etc)* el horario *[orar-yo]*
open top *(car)* descapotable *[—ablay]*
opera la ópera
operation *(med)* una operación *[opairathyon]*
operator *(tel)* la operadora
opportunity una oportunidad *[—too—]*
opposite: opposite the church enfrente de la iglesia; **it's directly opposite** está justo enfrente *[hoosto]*
oppressive *(heat)* sofocante
optician óptico
optimistic optimista
optional optativo *[—eebo]*
or o
orange *(fruit)* una naranja *[naran-ha]*; *(colour)* color naranja
orange juice *(fresh)* zumo de naranja

[thoomo]; *(fizzy, diluted)* naranjada *[naran-hada]*
orchestra la orquesta *[orkesta]*
order: could we order now? ¿podemos pedir ya?; **I've already ordered** ya he pedido *[ya ay]*; **I didn't order that** no he pedido eso *[no ay ...]*; **it's out of order** *(elevator etc)* no funciona *[no foonth-yona]*
ordinary corriente *[korr-yentay]*
organization una organización *[—athyon]*
organize organizar *[organeethar]*; **could you organize it?** ¿puede organizarlo? *[pway-day]*
original original *[oree-heenal]*; **is it an original?** *(painting etc)* ¿es original?
ornament un adorno
ostentatious *(clothes, person)* pretencioso *[—thyoso]*
other: the other waiter el otro camarero; **the other one** el otro; **do you have any others?** ¿tiene usted más que estos? *[t-yenay oostay]*; *(different ones)* ¿tiene usted otros distintos?; **some other time, thanks** en otro momento, gracias
otherwise de otra manera
ouch! ¡ay! *[eye]*
ought: he ought to be here soon no creo que tarde *[no kray-o kay tarday]*
ounce una onza *[ontha] see page 118*
our nuestro *[nwestro] see page 103*
ours (el) nuestro *[nwestro] see page 107*
out: he's out *(of building etc)* no está; **get out!** ¡fuera! *[fwaira]*; **I'm out of money** no tengo dinero; **a few kilometres out of town** a unos kilómetros de la ciudad *[th-yooda]*
outboard *(motor)* un fuera-bordo
outdoors fuera de casa *[fwaira]*
outlet *(elec)* una toma de corriente
outside: can we sit outside? ¿podemos sentarnos fuera? *[fwaira]*
outskirts: on the outskirts of ... en las afueras de ... *[afwairas]*
oven el horno *[orno]*
over: over here por aquí *[akee]*; **over there** por allí *[ayee]*; **over 100** más de 100; **I'm burnt all over** estoy todo quemado; **the holiday's over** se acabaron las vacaciones *[bakath-yonays]*
overcharge: you've overcharged me me ha cobrado de más *[may a]*

overcoat un abrigo
overcooked quemado *[kaymado]*
overdrive la sobremarcha
overexposed sobreexpuesto *[sobray-espwesto]*
overheat: it's overheating (*car*) se calienta *[say kal-yenta]*
overland por tierra *[t-yairra]*
overlook: overlooking the sea con vistas al mar *[kon beestas]*
overnight (*travel*) de noche

oversleep: I overslept se me han pegado las sábanas *[say may an]*
overtake adelantar
overweight (*person*) gordo
owe: how much do I owe you? ¿cuánto le debo? *[kwanto]*
own: my own ... mi propio ...; **are you on your own?** ¿está solo?; **I'm on my own** estoy solo
owner el propietario
oyster una ostra

P

pack: a pack of cigarettes un paquete de cigarrillos *[pakay-tay day theegaree-yos]*; **I'll go and pack** iré a hacer las maletas *[eeray a athair]*
package un paquete *[pakay-tay]*
package holiday, package tour un viaje organizado *[b-yaHay organeethado]*
packed lunch una bolsa con la comida
packed out: the place was packed out el sitio estaba lleno *[yayno]*
packet (*parcel*) un paquete *[pakay-tay]*; **a packet of cigarettes** un paquete de cigarrillos *[pakay-tay day theegaree-yos]*
paddle el remo
padlock un candado
page (*of book*) la página *[pa-Heena]*; **could you page him?** ¿podría llamarle? *[po-dree-a yamarlay]*
pain un dolor; **I have a pain here** me duele aquí *[may dway-lay akee]*
painful doloroso
painkillers unos calmantes
paint la pintura; **I'm going to do some painting** voy a pintar *[boy]*
paintbrush (*for wall*) una brocha; (*picture*) un pincel *[peenthel]*
painting un cuadro *[kwadro]*
pair: a pair of ... un par de ...
pajamas el pijama *[pee-Hama]*
Pakistan Paquistán *[pakeestan]*
Pakistani paquistaní *[pakeestanee]*
pal el amigote

palace el palacio *[palath-yo]*
pale pálido; **pale blue** azul claro *[athool]*
palm tree la palmera
palpitations las palpitaciones *[pal-peetath-yones]*
panic: don't panic! ¡con calma!
panties las bragas
pants (*trousers*) los pantalones; (*underpants*) los calzoncillos *[kalthon-theeyos]*
panty girdle una faja *[fa-Ha]*
pantyhose los panties
paper el papel; (*newspaper*) un periódico; **a piece of paper** un trozo de papel *[throtho]*
paper handkerchiefs kleenex (*tm*)
paraffin la parafina
paragliding el paragliding
parallel: parallel to ... paralelo a ...
parasol (*over table*) un parasol
parcel un paquete *[pakay-tay]*
pardon (me)? (*didn't understand*) ¿cómo?
parents: my parents mis padres
parents-in-law los suegros *[swaygros]*
park el parque *[parkay]*; **where can I park?** ¿dónde puedo aparcar el coche? *[donday pway-do]*; **there's nowhere to park** no hay dónde aparcar *[no eye]*
parka un anorak
parking lights las luces de estacionamiento *[loothays day estath-yonam-yento]*
parking lot un aparcamiento

parking place: there's a parking place!
¡allí hay un sitio para aparcar! *[ayee eye oon seet-yo]*

part una parte

partner el compañero *[kompan-yairo]*; (*at dinner etc*) la pareja *[paray-Ha]*; (*business*) el socio *[soth-yo]*

party (*group*) un grupo *[groopo]*; (*celebration*) una fiesta; **let's have a party** hagamos una fiesta *[agamos]*

pass (*mountain*) el puerto *[pwairto]*; (*overtake*) adelantar; **he passed out** ha perdido el conocimiento *[a pairdeedo el konotheem-yento]*; **he made a pass at me** intentó propasarse

passable (*road*) transitable *[—ablay]*

passenger un pasajero *[passa-Hairo]*

passport el pasaporte

past: in the past antiguamente *[anteegwa-mentay]*; **just past the bank** justo después del banco *[Hoosto despways] see page 116*

pastry la masa; (*cake*) una tarta; (*small cake*) un pastel

patch: could you put a patch on this? ¿podría ponerle un parche a esto?

pâté el paté *[patay]*

path un camino

patient: be patient tenga paciencia *[path-yenth-ya]*

patio el patio

pattern (*on cloth etc*) el dibujo *[deeboo-Ho]*; **a dress pattern** un patrón

paunch la barriga

pavement (*sidewalk*) la acera *[athaira]*

pay pagar; **can I pay, please?** la cuenta, por favor *[kwenta]*; **it's already paid for** ya está pagado; **I'll pay for this** (*at a meal etc*) pago yo

pay phone una cabina telefónica

peace and quiet paz y tranquilidad *[path ee trankeeleeda]*

peach un melocotón

peanuts cacahuetes *[kaka-waytays]*

pear una pera

pearl una perla

peas guisantes *[gees-antays]*

peculiar (*taste, custom etc*) raro *[ra-ro]*

pedal un pedal

pedalo un hidropedal *[eedro—]*

pedestrian un peatón *[pay-aton]*

pedestrian crossing un paso de peatones *[pay-atonays]*

pedestrian precinct una calle para peatones *[kayay para pay-atonays]*

pee: I need to go for a pee necesito hacer pis *[netheseeto athair pees]*

peeping Tom un voyeur

peg (*for washing*) una pinza *[peentha]*; (*for tent*) la estaca

pen una pluma *[plooma]*; **do you have a pen?** ¿tiene una pluma? *[t-yenay]*

pencil un lápiz *[lapeeth]*

pen friend un amigo por correspondencia *[korrespondenth-ya]*; **shall we be pen-friends?** ¿quieres que seamos amigos por correspondencia? *[k-yairays kay say-amos]*

penicillin la penicilina *[peneetheeleena]*

penknife una navaja *[nava-Ha]*

pen pal un amigo por correspondencia *[korrespondenth-ya]*

pensioner un pensionista *[penss-yoneesta]*

people la gente *[Hentay]*; **lot of people** mucha gente; **Spanish people** los españoles

pepper (*spice*) la pimienta *[peem-yenta]*; **green pepper** un pimiento verde *[bairday]*; **red pepper** un pimiento rojo *[ro-Ho]*

peppermint (*sweet*) un caramelo de menta

per: per night por noche; **how much per hour?** ¿cuánto cuesta por hora? *[kwanto kwesta por ora]*

per cent por ciento *[th-yento]*

perfect perfecto *[pairfecto]*

perfume el perfume *[pairfoomay]*

perhaps quizás *[keethass]*

period el período *[pairee-odo]*

perm una permanente *[pair—]*

permit un permiso *[pair—]*

person una persona *[pair—]*

pessimist(ic) pesimista

petrol la gasolina

petrol can un bidón de gasolina

petrol station una gasolinera

petrol tank el depósito de gasolina

pharmacy una farmacia *[farmath-ya]*

phone *see* **telephone**

photogenic fotogénico *[foto-Heneeko]*

photograph una foto; **would you take a photograph of us?** ¿le importaría hacernos una foto? *[lay eemportaree-a athair-nos]*

photographer el fotógrafo
phrase: a useful phrase una frase útil *[frasay ooteel]*
phrasebook un libro de frases
pianist un/una pianista
piano un piano
pickpocket un carterista
pick up: when can I pick them up? ¿cuándo puedo recogerlos? *[kwando pway-do rayko-наirlos]*; **will you come and pick me up?** ¿vendrás a recogerme? *[bendras a rayko-наirmay]*
picnic un picnic
picture un cuadro *[kwadro]*
pie (*meat*) una empanada; (*small*) una empanadilla; (*fruit*) una tarta
piece un pedazo *[pedatho]*; **a piece of ...** un pedazo de ...
pig un cerdo *[thairdo]*
pigeon una paloma
piles (*med*) hemorroides *[emo-rroydays]*
pile-up un accidente múltiple *[aktheedentay moolteeplay]*
pill una píldora; **I'm on the pill** estoy tomando la píldora
pillarbox un buzón *[boothon]*
pillow una almohada *[almo-ada]*
pillow case una funda (de almohada)
pin un alfiler *[alfeel-air]*
pineapple una piña *[peen-ya]*
pineapple juice un zumo de piña *[thoomo]*
pink rosa
pint una pinta *[peenta]* see page 119
pipe un tubo *[toobo]*; (*smoking*) una pipa
pipe cleaners unos limpiapipas *[le-empya—]*
pipe tobacco el tabaco de pipa
pity: it's a pity es una lástima
pizza una pizza *[peesa]*
place un sitio *[seet-yo]*; **is this place taken?** ¿está ocupado este sitio?; **would you keep my place for me?** ¿me guarda el sitio? *[may gwarda el seet-yo]*; **at my place** en mi casa
place mat un mantel individual *[een-deebeed-wal]*
plain (*food*) sencilla *[sen-theeya]*; (*not patterned*) liso
plane un avión *[ab-yon]*
plant una planta
plaster cast una escayola *[eska-yola]*
plastic plástico

plastic bag una bolsa de plástico
plate un plato
platform el andén; **which platform, please?** ¿qué andén, por favor? *[kay]*
play jugar *[ноogar]*; (*in theatre*) una obra
playboy un playboy
playground el patio de recreo *[ray-krayo]*
pleasant agradable *[—dablay]*
please: could you please ...? ¿podría hacer el favor de ...? *[podree-a athair el fabor day]*; **yes please** sí, por favor *[por fabor]*
plenty: plenty of ... mucho ... *[moocho]*; **that's plenty thanks** es suficiente, gracias *[soofeeth-yentay]*
pleurisy pleuresía *[play-ooresee-a]*
pliers unos alicates *[aleekatays]*
plonk vino malo *[beeno]*
plug (*elec*) un enchufe *[enchoofay]*; (*car*) una bujía *[boo-нee-a]*; (*bathroom*) el tapón
plughole el desagüe *[desag-way]*
plum una ciruela *[theer-wayla]*
plumber el fontanero
plus más
p.m. de la tarde
pneumonia pulmonía *[poolmonee-a]*
poached egg un huevo escalfado *[waybo]*
pocket el bolsillo *[bolsee-yo]*; **in my pocket** en mi bolsillo
pocketbook (*woman's*) el monedero
pocketknife una navaja *[naba-на]*
point: could you point to it? ¿puede señalarlo? *[pway-day senyalarlo]*; **four point six** cuatro coma seis *[kwatro koma says]*; **there's no point** no merece la pena *[no mair-ethay]*
points (*car*) los platinos
poisonous venenoso *[ben—]*
police la policía *[poleethee-a]*; **call the police!** llame a la policía *[yamay]*
policeman un (agente de) policía *[a-нentay]*
police station la comisaría de policía *[—ree-a]*
polish el betún *[betoon]*; **will you polish my shoes?** ¿puede limpiarme los zapatos? *[thapatos]*
polite educado *[edookado]*
politician un político
politics la política
polluted contaminado

pond un estanque *[estan-kay]*
pony un poney
pool (*swimming*) una piscina *[peess-theena]*
pool table la mesa de billar *[bee-yar]*
poor (*not rich*) pobre *[pobray]*; (*quality etc*) de baja calidad *[baнa]*; **poor old Manuel!** ¡pobre Manuel!
Pope el Papa
pop music la música pop
pop singer un cantante de música pop
popular popular *[popoolar]*
population la población *[poblath-yon]*
pork carne de cerdo *[karnay day thairdo]*
port (*for boats*) un puerto *[pwairto]*; (*drink*) un Oporto
porter (*hotel*) el conserje *[konsair-нay]*; (*for luggage*) un mozo *[motho]*
portrait un retrato
Portugal Portugal *[portoogal]*
Portuguese (*man*) un portugués *[portoogays]*; (*woman*) una portuguesa; (*language*) portugués
poser (*phoney person*) una persona falsa
posh (*restaurant*) de lujo *[loo-нo]*; (*people*) snob *[essnob]*
possibility la posibilidad *[—eeda]*
possible posible *[poseeblay]*; **is it possible to ...?** ¿es posible ...?; **as ... as possible** tan ... como sea posible *[say-a]*
post (*mail*) el correo *[korray-o]*; **could you post this for me?** ¿podría enviarme esto por correo? *[podree-a emb-yar]*
postbox un buzón *[boothon]*
postcard una postal
poster un poster
poste restante la lista de Correos
post office Correos *[korray-os]*
pot una olla *[oya]*; **a pot of tea** una tetera; **pots and pans** cacharros de cocina *[kotheena]*
potato una patata
potato chips patatas fritas
potato salad ensalada de patatas
pottery cerámica *[therameeka]*
pound (*money, weight*) una libra *see page 118*
pour: it's pouring down está lloviendo a cántaros *[esta yob-yendo]*
powder (*for face*) polvos para la cara *[polbos]*
powdered milk la leche en polvo *[lechay em polbo]*

power cut un apagón
power point una toma de corriente *[korr-yentay]*
power station una central eléctrica *[thentral]*
practise, practice: I need to practise necesito practicar *[neth—]*
pram un cochecito *[kochay-theeto]*
prawn cocktail un cocktail de gambas
prawns gambas
prefer: I prefer white wine prefiero el vino blanco *[pref-yairo]*
preferably: preferably not tomorrow de preferencia que no sea mañana *[day preferenth-ya]*
pregnant embarazada *[embarathada]*
prescription una receta *[ray-thayta]*
present: at present actualmente *[aktwalmentay]*; **here's a present for you** le traigo un regalo *[lay try-go]*
president el presidente
press: could you press these? ¿puede planchármelos? *[pway-day plancharmay-los]*
pretty mono; **it's pretty expensive** es bastante caro
price el precio *[preth-yo]*
prickly heat sarpullido
priest un sacerdote *[sathair-dotay]*
prime minister el primer ministro
print (*picture*) una foto
printed matter impresos
priority (*in driving*) **who has priority?** ¿quién tiene preferencia? *[k-yen t-yenay prefairenth-ya]*
prison la cárcel *[karthel]*
private privado *[preebado]*; **private bath** un baño privado *[ban-yo preebado]*
prize el premio
probably probablemente *[probablay-mentay]*
problem un problema; **I have a problem** tengo un problema; **no problem** con mucho gusto *[goosto]*
product un producto *[prodookto]*
program(me) el programa
promise: I promise lo prometo; **is that a promise?** ¿es una promesa?
pronounce: how do you pronounce this word? ¿cómo se pronuncia esta palabra? *[komo say pronoonth-ya]*
properly: it's not repaired properly no está bien arreglado

prostitute una prostituta *[—toota]*
protect proteger *[proteнair]*
protection factor el factor de protección
  [protekth-yon]
protein remover (*for contact lenses*) unas
  pastillas para limpiar las lentillas *[pas-*
  tee-yas para leemp-yar las lentee-yas]
Protestant protestante
proud orgulloso *[orgoo-yoso]*
prunes las ciruelas pasas *[theer-waylas]*
public público *[poobleeko]*
public convenience los aseos públicos
  [assayos]
public holiday un día de fiesta
pudding (*dessert*) el postre *[postray]*
pull tirar de; **he pulled out without indi-
cating** salió sin indicar *[sal-yo]*
pullover un jersey *[наirsay]*
pump la bomba
punctual puntual *[poont-wal]*
puncture un pinchazo *[peenchatho]*

pure puro *[pooro]*
purple morado
purse el monedero; (*handbag*) el bolso
push empujar *[empoo-наr]*; **don't push
in!** ¡(*into queue*) ¡no se cuele! *[no say kway-
lay]*
push-chair una sillita de ruedas *[see-
yeeta day rwaydas]*
put: where did you put ...? ¿dónde ha
  puesto...? *[pwesto]*; **where can I put...?**
  ¿dónde puedo poner ...? *[donday pway-
do pon-air]*; **could you put the lights
on?** ¿podría encender las luces *[podree-a
enthendair las loothays]*; **will you put
the light out?** ¿podría apagar la luz?
[looth]; **you've put the price up** ha
  subido los precios *[a soobeedo los preth-
yos]*; **could you put us up for a night?**
¿podría alojarnos por una noche? *[po-
dree-a alo-наrnos]*
pyjamas el pijama *[pee-наma]*

Q

quality la calidad *[kaleeda]*; **poor quality**
  de mala calidad; **good quality** de buena
  calidad *[bwena]*
quarantine la cuarentena *[kwarentay-
na]*
quart *see page 119*
quarter la cuarta parte *[kwarta partay]*; **a
quarter of an hour** un cuarto de hora
[kwarto day ora] see page 116
quay el muelle *[mwe-yay]*
quayside: on the quayside en el muelle
  [mwe-yay]
question una pregunta *[pregoonta]*;
  that's out of the question es imposible

[—eeblay]
queue una cola; **there was a big queue**
  había una cola larga *[abee-a]*
quick rápido; **that was quick** sí que ha
  sido rápido *[see kay a]*; **which is the
quickest way?** ¿cuál es el camino más
rápido? *[kwal]*
quickly rapidamente
quiet (*place, hotel*) tranquilo *[trankeelo]*;
  be quiet! ¡cállese! *[ka-yay-say]*
quinine la quinina *[keeneena]*
quite: quite a lot bastante; **it's quite
different** es muy diferente *[mwee]*; **I'm
not quite sure** no estoy muy seguro

R

rabbit un conejo *[konay-HO]*
rabies la rabia *[rab-ya]*
race (*horses, cars*) una carrera *[karraira]*;
  I'll race you there te echo una carrera
  [tay aycho]
racket (*tennis etc*) una raqueta *[rakay-ta]*
radiator el radiador *[rad-yador]*
radio la radio *[rad-yo]*; **on the radio** por
  la radio
rag (*cleaning*) un trapo
rail: by rail en tren
railroad, railway el ferrocarril
railroad crossing un paso a nivel
  [neebel]
rain la lluvia *[yoob-ya]*; **in the rain** bajo la
  lluvia *[ba-HO]*; **it's raining** está lloviendo
  [yob-yendo]
rain boots unas botas de agua *[day
  ag-wa]*
raincoat un impermeable *[eempairmay-
  ablay]*
rape una violación *[b-yolath-yon]*
rare poco común *[komoon]*; (*steak*) (muy)
  poco hecho *[(mwee) ... aycho]*
rash (*on skin*) una erupción cutánea *[ai-
  roopth-yon kootanay-a]*
raspberries unas frambuesas *[frambway-
  sas]*
rat una rata
rate (*for changing money*) el cambio; **what's
  the rate for the pound?** ¿a cuánto está la
  libra? *[a kwanto]*; **what are your rates?**
  (*car hire etc*) ¿cuáles son sus tarifas? *[kwa-
  lays]*
rather: it's rather late es algo tarde; **I'd
  rather have fish** prefiero pescado *[pref-
  yairo]*
raw crudo *[kroodo]*
razor una maquinilla de afeitar *[ma-
  keenee-ya day afay-tar]*; (*electric*) una máquina de afeitar eléctrica *[makeena]*
razor blades cuchillas de afeitar *[koo-
  cheeyas]*
reach: within easy reach de fácil alcance

[day fatheel alkanthay]
read leer *[lay-air]*; **I can't read it** no lo
  puedo leer *[... pway-do ...]*
ready: when will it be ready? ¿cuándo
  estará listo? *[kwando]*; **I'll go and get
  ready** iré a prepararme *[iray]*; **I'm not
  ready yet** aún no estoy listo *[a-oon]*
real verdadero *[bairdadairo]*
really realmente *[ray-almentay]*; **I really
  must go** de verdad que tengo que irme
  [day bairda kay tengo kay irmay]; **is it
  really necessary?** ¿es realmente necesario? *[nethesar-yo]*
realtor un agente inmobiliario *[a-Hen-
  tay]*
rear: at the rear en la parte trasera; **rear
  wheels** las ruedas traseras *[rway-das]*
rearview mirror el (espejo) retrovisor
  [espay-HO retrobeesor]
reason: the reason is that ... el motivo es
  que ... *[moteebo]*
reasonable razonable *[rathona-blay]*
receipt un recibo *[rethee-bo]*
recently recientemente *[reth-yentay-
  mentay]*
reception (*hotel*) la recepción *[rethepth-
  yon]*
reception desk la recepción *[rethepth-
  yon]*
receptionist el/la recepcionista
  [rethepth-yoneesta]
recipe una receta *[ray-thay-ta]*; **can you
  give me the recipe for this?** ¿me podría
  dar la receta? *[may podree-a]*
recognize reconocer *[rekonothair]*; **I
  didn't recognize it** no lo reconocí *[re-
  konothee]*
**recommend: could you recommend
  ...?** ¿puede usted recomendar ...? *[pway-
  day oostay]*
record (*music*) un disco
record player un tocadiscos
red rojo *[ro-HO]*
red wine vino tinto *[beeno]*

reduction (*in price*) un descuento [*des-kwento*]

refreshing refrescante

refrigerator el refrigerador [*refreeнairador*]

refund un reembolso [*ray-embolso*]

region una región [*re-нyon*]

registered: by registered mail por correo certificado [*korray-o thairteefeekado*]

registration number el número de la matrícula [*matreekoola*]

relative: my relatives mis parientes [*paryentays*]

relaxing: it's very relaxing es muy relajante [*rela-нantay*]

reliable (*person*) de confianza [*day konfyantha*]; (*car*) seguro [*segooro*]

religion la religión [*releeн-yon*]

remains (*of old city etc*) las ruinas [*rweenas*]

remember: I don't remember no recuerdo [*rekwairdo*]; **do you remember?** ¿recuerda? [*rekwairda*]

remote (*village etc*) remoto

rent el alquiler [*alkeelair*]; **I'd like to rent a bike/car** quisiera alquilar una bicicleta/un coche [*kees-yaira alkeelar*]

rental car un coche alquilado [*alkeelado*]

repair reparar; **can you repair this?** ¿puede arreglarlo? [*pway-day*]

repeat: could you repeat that? ¿puede repetir esto? [*pway-day*]

representative (*of company*) el representante

rescue rescatar

reservation una reserva [*ressairba*]; **I have a reservation** tengo una reserva

reserve reservar [*ressairbar*]; **I reserved a room in the name of ...** reservé una habitación a nombre de ... [*ressairbay*]; **can I reserve a table for tonight?** ¿puedo reservar una mesa para esta noche? [*pway-do resairbar*]

rest: I need a rest necesito un descanso [*nethesseeto*]; **the rest of the group** el resto del grupo

restaurant un restaurante [*rest-owrantay*]

rest room los aseos [*assay-os*]

retired: I'm retired estoy jubilado [*ноobeelado*]

return: a return to Barcelona un billete de ida y vuelta a Barcelona [*beeyay-tay day eeda ee bwelta*]; **I'll return it tomorrow** lo devolveré mañana [*daybolbairay*]

returnable (*deposit*) reembolsable [*rayembolsablay*]

reverse charge call una llamada a cobro revertido [*yamada a kobro rebarteedo*]

reverse gear la marcha atrás

revolting (*taste, food etc*) asqueroso [*askayroso*]

rheumatism el reumatismo [*ray-oomateezmo*]

rib una costilla [*kosteeya*]; **a cracked rib** una costilla rota

ribbon (*for hair*) una cinta [*theenta*]

rice arroz [*arroth*]

rich (*person*) rico; **it's too rich** (*food*) está demasiado fuerte [*fwairtay*]

ride: can you give me a ride into town? ¿puede llevarme en su coche a la ciudad? [*pway-day yay-barmay ... th-yooda*]; **thanks for the ride** gracias por traerme [*tra-airmay*]

ridiculous: that's ridiculous! ¡es ridículo! [*reedeekoolo*]

right (*correct*) correcto; (*not left*) derecho; **you're right** tiene razón [*t-yenay rathon*]; **you were right** tenía razón [*tenee-a*]; **that's right** eso es; **that can't be right** eso no puede ser así [*pway-day sair assee*]; **right!** (*ok*) ¡bien! [*b-yen*]; **is this the right road for ...?** ¿es éste el camino correcto para ir a ...?; **on the right** a la derecha; **turn right** gire a la derecha [*нeeray*]; **not right now** no en este momento

righthand drive con el volante a la derecha [*bolantay*]

ring (*on finger*) una sortija [*sortee-нa*]; (*on cooker, gas ring*) el hornillo [*ornee-yo*]; **I'll ring you** te llamaré [*tay yamaray*]

ring road la carretera de circunvalación [*theerkoombalath-yon*]

ripe maduro [*madooro*]

rip-off: it's a rip-off es un timo; **rip-off prices** precios altísimos [*preth-yos*]

risky arriesgado [*arr-yezgado*]; **it's too risky** es demasiado arriesgado

river un río [*ree-o*]; **by the river** a orillas del río [*oree-yas*]

road la carretera; **is this the road to ...?** ¿es ésta la carretera que va a ...?; **further**

down the road más adelante
road accident un accidente automovi-
lístico [aktheedentay owtomobee-
leesteeko]
road hog un loco del volante [bolantay]
road map un mapa de carreteras
roadside: by the roadside al borde del
camino [borday]
roadsign una señal de carretera [sen-yal]
roadwork(s) obras
roast beef un roast beef
rob: I've been robbed! ¡me han robado!
[may an]
robe (housecoat) una bata
rock (stone) una roca; **on the rocks** (with
ice) con hielo [yaylo]
rocky (coast) rocosa
roll (bread) un panecillo [pan-etheeyo]
Roman Catholic católico
romance un romance [romanthay]
Rome: when in Rome ... donde fueres
haz lo que vieres [donday fway-rays ath
lo kay b-yairays]
roof el tejado [teнado]; **on the roof** en el
tejado
roof rack la baca
room una habitación [abeetath-yon]; **do
you have a room?** ¿tiene una habitación? [t-yenay]; **a room for two people**
una habitación para dos; **a room for
three nights** una habitación para tres
noches [notchays]; **a room with bathroom** una habitación con baño [ban-yo];
in my room en mi cuarto [kwarto]; **there's no room** no hay sitio [no eye seet-
yo]
room service el servicio de habitaciones
[sair-beeth-yo day abeetath-yonays]
rope una cuerda [kwair-da]
rose una rosa [rossa]
rosé (wine) vino rosado [beeno]
rotary (for traffic) un cruce en glorieta
[kroothay]

rough (sea, crossing) revuelto [rebwelto];
the engine sounds a bit rough el motor
no suena bien [swayna b-yen]; **I've been
sleeping rough** (in open air) he estado
durmiendo a la intemperie [doorm-
yendo a la eentempair-yay]
roughly (approximately) aproximadamente
roulette la ruleta
round (adjective) redondo; **it's my round**
es mi turno [toorno]
roundabout (traffic) un cruce en glorieta
[kroothay en glor-yayta]
round-trip: a round-trip ticket to ... un
billete de ida y vuelta a ... [oom beeyay-
tay day eeda ee bwelta]
route una ruta [roota]; **what's the best
route?** ¿cuál es la mejor ruta? [kwal es la
me-нor]
rowboat, rowing boat un barco de remos
rubber (material) la goma; (eraser) una
goma de borrar
rubber band una goma elástica
rubbish (waste) la basura [basoora]; (poor
quality items) porquerías [porkairee-as];
rubbish! ¡tonterías! [tontairee-as]
rucksack una mochila
rude grosero; **he was very rude** fue muy
grosero [fway mwee]
rug una alfombra
ruins (of ancient city etc) las ruinas
[rweenas]
rum un ron
rum and coke un cubalibre
run (person) correr [korrair]; **I go running**
corro; **quick, run!** ¡de prisa, corre! [ko-
rray]; **how often do the buses run?**
¿cada cuánto pasan los autobuses? [kada
kwanto ... owtobooses]; **he's been run
over** ha sido atropellado [atrop-eyado];
I've run out of gas/petrol se me ha
acabado la gasolina [say may a]
rupture (med) una hernia [airn-ya]
Russia Rusia [roos-ya]

S

saccharine la sacarina
sad triste
saddle (*horse*) la silla de montar *[see-ya]*; (*bicycle*) el sillín *[see-yeen]*
safe seguro *[segooro]*; **will it be safe here?** ¿estará seguro aquí? *[akee]*; **is it safe to drink?** ¿se puede beber? *[say pway-day bebair]*; **is it a safe beach for swimming?** ¿se puede nadar sin peligro? *[say pway-day]*; **could you put this in your safe?** ¿podría guardarme esto en la caja fuerte? *[podree-a gwardarmay ... ka-нa fwairtay]*
safety pin un imperdible *[eempairdee-blay]*
sail una vela *[bayla]*; **can we go sailing?** ¿podemos hacer vela? *[... ath-air ...]*
sailboard el windsurfing
sailboarding: I like sailboarding me gusta el windsurfing
sailor (*navy*) un marinero; (*sport*) un marino
salad una ensalada
salad cream la mayonesa
salad dressing el aliño para la ensalada *[aleen-yo]*
sale: is it for sale? ¿está en venta? *[em benta]*; **it's not for sale** no está en venta
sales clerk el dependiente *[depend-yentay]*
salmon el salmón *[sal-mon]*
salt la sal
salty: it's too salty está demasiado salado
same mismo *[meez-mo]*; **one the same as this** uno igual a éste *[eegwal]*; **the same again, please** lo mismo otra vez, por favor *[... beth ...]*; **have a good day — same to you** ¡qué tenga un buen día! — usted también *[oostay tamb-yen]*; **it's all the same to me** me es igual *[may es eegwal]*; **thanks all the same** gracias de todas maneras
sand la arena *[arayna]*

sandal una sandalia *[sandal-ya]*; **a pair of sandals** un par de sandalias
sandwich un sandwich; **a chicken sandwich** un sandwich de pollo *[po-yo]*
sandy (*beach*) arenoso
sanitary napkin, sanitary towel una compresa
sarcastic sarcástico
sardines las sardinas
satisfactory satisfactorio; **this is not satisfactory** no es satisfactorio
Saturday el sábado
sauce la salsa
saucepan un cazo *[katho]*
saucer un platillo *[plateeyo]*
sauna un sauna *[sowna]*
sausage una salchicha
saute potatoes unas patatas salteadas *[saltay-adas]*
save (*life*) salvar *[salbar]*
savo(u)ry salado
say: how do you say ... in Spanish? ¿cómo se dice ... en castellano? *[komo say deethay en kaste-yano]*; **what did he say?** ¿qué ha dicho? *[kay a deecho]*; **what did you say?** ¿qué ha dicho?; **I wouldn't say no** con mucho gusto
scald: he's scalded himself se ha quemado *[kemado]*
scarf una bufanda *[boofanda]*; (*head*) un pañuelo *[pan-yway-lo]*
scarlet rojo vivo *[ro-нo beebo]*
scenery el paisaje *[pye-saнay]*
scent (*perfume*) el perfume *[pairfoomay]*
schedule un programa
scheduled flight un vuelo regular *[bwaylo regoolar]*
school la escuela *[eskwayla]*; (*university*) la universidad *[ooneebairseeda]*; **I'm still at school** todavía voy al colegio *[toda-bee-a boy al koleнyo]*
science la ciencia *[th-yenth-ya]*
scissors: a pair of scissors unas tijeras

[tee-нairas]
scooter una moto
scorching: it's really scorching el sol está que quema *[kay kayma]*
score: what's the score? (*sport*) ¿quién va ganando? *[k-yen ba]*
scotch (whisky) un whisky escocés *[eskothays]*
Scotch tape (*tm*) una cinta adhesiva *[theenta ad-eseeba]*
Scotland Escocia *[eskoth-ya]*
Scottish escocés *[eskothays]*
scrambled eggs unos huevos revueltos *[waybos reb-weltos]*
scratch arañar *[aran-yar]*; **it's only a scratch** es sólo un rasguño *[razgoon-yo]*
scream un grito
screw un tornillo *[torneeyo]*
screwdriver un destornillador *[destorneeyador]*
scrubbing brush un cepillo de fregar *[thepee-yo]*
scruffy (*appearance*) andrajoso *[andra-нoso]*
scuba diving el buceo *[boothay-o]*
sea el mar; **by the sea** junto al mar *[нoonto]*
sea air el aire de mar *[eye-ray]*
seafood los mariscos
seafood restaurant una marisquería *[mareeskairee-a]*
seafront: on the seafront en frente de la playa *[ply-a]*
seagull una gaviota *[gab-yota]*
search buscar *[booskar]*; **I searched everywhere** busqué por todas partes *[booskay]*
search party una expedición de búsqueda *[espedeeth-yon day booskayda]*
seashell una concha marina
seasick: I feel seasick estoy mareado *[maray-ado]*; **I get seasick** me mareo *[may maray-o]*
seaside: by the seaside cerca de la playa *[thairka day la ply-a]*; **let's go to the seaside** vamos a la playa *[bamos]*
season la temporada; **in the high season** en la temporada alta; **in the low season** en la temporada baja *[ba-нa]*
seasoning el condimento
seat el asiento *[as-yento]*; **is this anyone's seat?** ¿está ocupado este asiento? *[... okoopado ...]*

seat belt el cinturón de seguridad *[theentooron day segooreeda]*; **do you have to wear a seatbelt?** ¿hay que usar el cinturón de seguridad? *[eye kay oosar]*
sea urchin un erizo de mar *[airee-tho]*
seaweed las algas
secluded apartado
second (*adjective*) segundo *[segoondo]*; (*time*) un segundo; **just a second!** ¡un momento!; **can I have a second helping?** ¿puedo servirme otra vez? *[pway-do sairbeermay otra beth]*
second class (*travel*) en segunda clase
second-hand de segunda mano
secret secreto *[say-krayto]*
security check un registro *[re-нeestro]*
sedative un calmante
see ver *[bair]*; **I didn't see it** no lo ví *[bee]*; **have you seen my husband?** ¿ha visto a mi marido? *[a beesto]*; **I saw him this morning** le ví esta mañana *[bee]*; **can I see the manager?** ¿puedo hablar con el gerente? *[pway-do ablar]*; **see you tonight!** ¡hasta la noche! *[asta]*; **can I see?** ¿puedo ver? *[pway-do bair]*; **oh, I see** ¡ah, ya comprendo!; **will you see to it?** ¿se encarga de hacerlo? *[athairlo]*
seldom rara vez *[beth]*
self-catering apartment un apartamento
self-service autoservicio *[owto-sairbeeth-yo]*
sell vender *[bendair]*; **do you sell ...?** ¿vende ...? *[benday]*; **will you sell it to me?** ¿me lo vende? *[may lo benday]*
sellotape (*tm*) un papel celo *[pap-el thaylo]*
send enviar *[emb-yar]*; **I want to send this to ...** quiero enviar esto a ... *[k-yairo emb-yar]*; **I'll have to send this food back** la comida está mala, llévesela *[komeeda ... yaybaysayla]*
senior: Mr Jones senior el señor Jones, padre
senior citizen un pensionista *[pens-yoneesta]*
sensational sensacional *[sensath-yonal]*
sense: I have no sense of direction no tengo buen sentido de la orientación *[... bwen ... or-yentath-yon]*; **it doesn't make sense** no tiene sentido *[no t-yenay]*
sensible razonable *[rathonablay]*
sensitive sensible *[senseeblay]*

sentimental sentimental

separate separado; **can we have separate bills?** queremos cuentas separadas, por favor *[kairay-mos kwentas]*

separated: I'm separated estoy separado

separately por separado

September septiembre *[sept-yembray]*

septic séptico

serious serio *[sairyo]*; **I'm serious** lo digo en serio; **you can't be serious!** ¡estás bromeando! *[bromay-ando]*; **is it serious, doctor?** ¿es grave, doctor? *[grabay]*

seriously: he's seriously ill está muy enfermo *[mwee enfairmo]*

service: the service was excellent el servicio ha sido excelente *[el sair-beeth-yo a seedo esthe-lentay]*; **could we have some service, please!** ¡nos podría atender, por favor! *[nos podree-a atendair]*; **(church) service** el culto; *(Catholic)* la misa; **the car needs a service** el coche necesita una revisión *[netheseeta oona rebees-yon]*

service charge el servicio *[sairbeeth-yo]*

service station una estación de servicio *[estath-yon day sair-beeth-yo]*

serviette una servilleta *[sair-beey-ayta]*

set: it's time we were setting off es hora de marcharnos *[ora day]*

set menu el menú del día *[menoo]*

settle up: can we settle up now? la cuenta, por favor *[kwenta]*

several varios *[bar-yos]*

sew: could you sew this back on? ¿podría coserme esto? *[kosairmay]*

sex *(activity)* el amor

sexist machista

sexy sexy

shade: in the shade a la sombra

shadow la sombra

shake: to shake hands estrecharse las manos *[... —say ...]*

shallow poco profundo *[profoondo]*

shame: what a shame! ¡qué lástima! *[kay]*

shampoo el champú *[champoo]*; **can I have a shampoo and set?** quiero un lavado y marcado *[k-yairo oon labado]*; **can I have a shampoo and blow-dry?** quiero un lavado y secado a mano

shandy una cerveza con limonada *[thairbaytha]*

share *(room, table)* compartir; **let's share the cost** compartamos el costo

shark un tiburón *[teebooron]*

sharp *(knife etc)* afilado; *(taste)* ácido *[atheedo]*; *(pain)* agudo *[agoodo]*

shattered: I'm shattered *(very tired)* estoy agotado

shave: I need a shave necesito un afeitado *[nethesseeto oon afay-tado]*; **can you give me a shave?** ¿podría afeitarme? *[podree-a afay-tarmay]*

shaver una máquina de afeitar *[makeena day afay-tar]*

shaving brush una brocha de afeitar *[afay-tar]*

shaving foam la espuma de afeitar *[afay-tar]*

shaving point el enchufe para la máquina de afeitar *[enchoofay para la makeena day afay-tar]*

shaving soap el jabón de afeitar *[Habon day afay-tar]*

shawl un chal

she ella *[eya]*; **is she staying here?** ¿se hospeda aquí? *[say ospayda akee]*; **is she a friend of yours?** ¿es amiga suya? *[sooya]*; **she left yesterday** se marchó ayer *[a-yair]*; **she's not English** no es inglesa *see page 105*

sheep una oveja *[obay-Ha]*

sheet una sábana

shelf una estantería

shell *(seashell)* una concha

shellfish los mariscos

sherry un jerez *[Haireth]*

shingles *(med)* herpes *[air-pays]*

ship un barco; **by ship** en barco

shirt un camisa; **a clean shirt** una camisa limpia *[leemp-ya]*

shit! ¡mierda! *[m-yairda]*

shock *(surprise)* un susto *[soosto]*; **I got an electric shock from the ...** me ha dado una descarga eléctrica el/la ... *[may]*

shock-absorber un amortiguador *[amorteeg-wador]*

shocking escandaloso

shoelaces unos cordones para zapatos *[thapatos]*

shoe polish un betún para zapatos *[baytoon para thapatos]*

shoes los zapatos *[thapatos]*; **a pair of shoes** un par de zapatos

shop una tienda *[t-yenda]*

shopping: I'm going shopping voy de compras [boy]

shop window el escaparate [—ratay]

shore (of sea, lake) la orilla [oreeya]

short (person) bajo [ba-HO]; (time) corto; **it's only a short distance** queda bastante cerca [kayda ... thairka]

short-change: you've short-changed me me ha devuelto de menos [may a debwelto]

short circuit un corto circuito [theerk-weeto]

shortcut un atajo [ata-HO]

shorts los pantalones cortos; (underwear) los calzoncillos [kalthonthee-yos]

should: what should I do? ¿qué hago? [kay ago]; **he shouldn't be long** no tardará mucho; **you should have told me** debiste habérmelo dicho [... abairmaylo ...]

shoulder el hombro [ombro]

shoulder blade el homoplato [omoplato]

shout gritar

show: could you show me? ¿puede enseñarmelo? [pway-day ensen-yarmaylo]; **does it show?** ¿se nota?; **we'd like to go to a show** nos gustaría ir a ver un espectáculo [... eer a bair ...]

shower (in bathroom) la ducha [doocha]; **with shower** con ducha

shower cap un gorro de baño [banyo]

show-off: don't be a show-off no sea presumido [no say-a]

shrimps (in Galicia) los camarones; (in the rest of Spain) quisquillas [keeskee-yas]

shrine (at roadside) un santuario

shrink: it's shrunk se ha encogido [say a enko-Heedo]

shut cerrar [thairrar]; **when do you shut?** ¿a qué hora cierran? [a kay ora thyairran]; **when do they shut?** ¿a qué hora cierran?; **it was shut** estaba cerrado; **I've shut myself out** he olvidado la llave [may ay olbeedado la yabay]; **shut up!** ¡a callar! [a ka-yar]

shutter (phot) el obturador [optoorador]; (on window) la contraventana [kontrabentana]

shutter release el disparador

shy tímido

sick enfermo [enfairmo]; **I think I'm going to be sick** (vomit) creo que voy a devolver [kray-o kay boy a daybolbair]

side el lado; (in game) el equipo [ekeepo]; **at the side of the road** al lado de la carretera; **the other side of town** al otro lado de la ciudad [th-yooda]

side lights las luces de posición [loothes day posseeth-yon]

side salad una ensalada aparte

side street una callejuela [ka-yay-Hwayla]

sidewalk la acera [athaira]

sidewalk cafe una terraza (de un café) [tairratha]

siesta la siesta

sight: the sights of ... los lugares de interés de ... [loogares day eenteress]

sightseeing: sightseeing tour un recorrido turístico [tooreesteeko]; **we're going sightseeing** vamos a hacer un recorrido turístico [bamos a athair]

sign (roadsign) una señal de tráfico [senyal]; (notice) un letrero [letrairo]; **where do I sign?** ¿dónde firmo?

signal: he didn't give a signal no hizo ninguna señal [no eetho]

signature la firma

signpost un letrero [letrairo]

silence el silencio [seelenth-yo]

silencer el silenciador [seelenth-yador]

silk la seda

silly: that's silly! ¡qué tontería!

silver la plata

silver foil un papel de aluminio

similar parecido [pa-retheedo]

simple sencillo [sentheeyo]

since: since yesterday desde ayer [dezday a-yair]; **since we got here** desde que llegamos aquí [dezday kay yegamos akee]

sincere sincero [seenthairo]

sing cantar

singer un cantante

single: a single room una habitación individual [abeetath-yon eendeebeedwal]; **a single to ...** un billete para ... [bee-yay-tay]; **I'm single** soy soltero [soltairo]

sink (kitchen) el fregadero; **it sank** se hundió [say oond-yo]

sir señor [sen-yor]; **excuse me, sir** disculpe, señor

sirloin un solomillo [solomee-yo]

sister: my sister mi hermana [mee airmana]

sister-in-law: my sister-in-law mi cuñada *[koon-yada]*
sit: may I sit here? ¿puedo sentarme aquí? *[pway-do sentarmay akee]*; **is anyone sitting here?** ¿está ocupado este asiento? *[as-yento]*
site un sitio *[seet-yo]*
sitting: the second sitting for lunch el segundo turno de comedor *[... toorno ...]*
situation la situación *[seetwath-yon]*
size el tamaño *[taman-yo]*; *(clothes)* la talla *[ta-ya]*
sketch un dibujo *[deeboo-HO]*
ski el esquí *[eskee]*
skid: I skidded he dado un patinazo *[ay dado oom pateenatho]*
skin la piel *[p-yel]*
skin-diving el buceo *[boothay-o]*; **I'm going skin-diving** voy a bucear *[boy]*
skinny flaco
skirt la falda
skull el cráneo *[kranay-o]*
sky el cielo *[th-yaylo]*
sleep: I can't sleep no puedo dormir *[no pway-do]*; **did you sleep well?** ¿durmió bien? *[doorm-yo b-yen]*; **I need a good sleep** necesito dormir bien *[netheseeto]*
sleeper *(rail)* un coche-cama
sleeping bag un saco de dormir
sleeping car un coche-cama
sleeping pill una pastilla para dormir *[pastee-ya]*
sleepy soñoliento *[sonyol-yento]*; **I'm feeling sleepy** tengo sueño *[sway-nyo]*
sleeve la manga
slice *(of bread, meat etc)* una rebanada
slide *(phot)* una diapositiva *[d-yapossee-teeba]*
slim *(adjective)* delgado; **I'm slimming** estoy adelgazando *[ad-elgathando]*
slip *(under dress)* la combinación *[—ath-yon]*; **I slipped** *(on pavement etc)* me resbalé *[may rezbalay]*
slipped disc un disco dislocado
slippery resbaladizo *[rezbaladeetho]*
slow despacio *[despath-yo]*; **slow down** más despacio
slowly despacio *[despath-yo]*; **could you say it slowly?** ¿podría decirlo más despacio? *[podree-a detheerlo mas despath-yo]*
small pequeño *[pay-kay-nyo]*
small change calderilla *[—eeya]*

smallpox la viruela *[beerway-la]*
smart *(clothes)* elegante
smashing fabuloso *[fabooloso]*
smell: there's a funny smell hay un olor raro *[eye]*; **what a lovely smell** ¡qué olor tan agradable! *[agradablay]*; **it smells** ¡apesta!
smile *(verb)* sonreír *[sonray-eer]*; *(noun)* una sonrisa
smoke el humo *[oomo]*; **do you smoke?** ¿fuma? *[fooma]*; **do you mind if I smoke?** ¿le importa si fumo?; **I don't smoke** no fumo
smooth *(surface)* liso; *(sea)* calmado
smoothy: he's a real smoothy es un zalamero *[thalamairo]*
snack: I'd just like a snack quiero un bocadillo solamente *[k-yairo oon bo-kadee-yo]*
snackbar una cafetería
snake una culebra *[koolay-bra]*
sneakers unas playeras *[ply-airas]*
snob un snob *[esnob]*
snorkel un tubo de buceo *[toobo de boothay-o]*
snow la nieve *[n-yay-bay]*
so: it's so hot hace tanto calor *[athay]*; **it was so beautiful!** ¡fue tan bonito! *[fway]*; **not so fast** no tan de prisa; **thank you so much** muchas gracias; **it wasn't — it was so!** no es cierto — claro que sí *[... th-yairto ...]*; **so am I** yo también; **so do I** yo también; **how was it? — so-so** ¿cómo estuvo? — así así *[... estoobo — asee asee]*
soaked: I'm soaked estoy empapado
soap el jabón *[Habon]*
soap-powder el jabón en polvo *[Habon em polbo]*
sober sobrio *[sobr-yo]*
soccer el fútbol
sock el calcetín *[kaltheteen]*
socket *(elec)* el enchufe *[enchoofay]*
soda (water) soda
sofa el sofá
soft suave *[swabay]*
soft drink un refresco
soldier un soldado
sole *(of shoe)* la suela *[sway-la]*; **could you put new soles on these?** ¿podría cambiarles las suelas? *[podree-a]*
solid sólido
some: may I have some water? ¿me da

un poco de **agua?**; **do you have some matches?** ¿tiene cerillas? *[t-yenay]*; **that's some drink!** ¡qué buena bebida! *[kay bwena]*; **some of them** algunos de ellos *[eyos]*; **can I have some?** ¿me da un poco? *[may]*; *(some of those)* ¿me da unos cuantos de ésos? *[... kwantos]*

somebody, someone alguien *[alg-yen]*

something algo; **something to drink** algo de beber

sometime: sometime this afternoon a alguna hora por la tarde *[a algoona ora]*

sometimes a veces *[a bethays]*

somewhere en alguna parte

son: my son mi hijo *[mee ee-Ho]*

song una canción *[kanth-yon]*

son-in-law el yerno *[yairno]*

soon pronto; **I'll be back soon** volveré pronto *[bolbair-ay]*; **as soon as you can** tan pronto como pueda *[pway-da]*

sore: it's sore me duele *[dway-lay]*

sore throat un dolor de garganta

sorry: (I'm) sorry perdone *[pairdonay]*; **sorry?** *(pardon)* ¿cómo?

sort: what sort of ...? ¿qué clase de ...? *[kay klassay day]*; **a different sort of ...** un ... difer*ente;* **will you sort it out?** ¿lo puede arreglar? *[pway-day]*

soup la sopa

sour *(taste, apple)* ácido *[atheedo]*

south el sur; **to the south** al sur

South Africa África del Sur

South African sudafricano

South America América del Sur

South American sudamericano

southeast el sudeste; **to the southeast** al sudeste

southwest el sudoeste *[soodo-estay]*; **to the southwest** al sudoeste

souvenir un recuerdo *[rek-wairdo]*

spa un balneario *[balnay-ar-yo]*

space heater un calentador eléctrico

spade una pala

Spain España *[espan-ya]*

Spaniard un español *[espan-yol]*

Spanish español *[espan-yol]*; *(language)* castellano *[kas-teyano]*; **a Spanish woman** una española; **the Spanish** los españoles

spanner una llave inglesa *[yabay]*

spare part un repuesto *[repwesto]*

spare tyre una rueda de repuesto *[rway-da]*

spark(ing) plug la bujía *[boo-Hee-a]*

speak: do you speak English? ¿habla inglés? *[abla]*; **I don't speak ...** no hablo ...; **can I speak to ...?** ¿puedo hablar con ...? *[pway-do]*; **speaking** *(telec)* soy yo, dígame *[deegamay]*

special especial *[espeth-yal]*; **nothing special** nada especial

specialist un especialista *[espeth-yaleesta]*

special(i)ty *(in restaurant)* la especialidad *[espeth-yaleeda]*; **the special(i)ty of the house** la especialidad de la casa

spectacles las gafas

speed la velocidad *[belotheeda]*; **he was speeding** iba demasiado rápido

speedboat un fuera borda *[fwaira]*

speed limit el límite de velocidad *[belotheeda]*

speedometer el velocímetro *[belotheemetro]*

spell: how do you spell it? ¿cómo se escribe? *[komo say eskreebay]*

spend: I've spent all my money he gastado todo mi dinero *[ay]*

spice una especia *[espeth-ya]*

spicy: it's very spicy está muy picante

spider una araña *[aranya]*

splendid espléndido

splint *(for broken limb)* una tablilla *[tableeya]*

splinter *(in finger etc)* una astilla *[asteeya]*

splitting: I've got a splitting headache tengo un terrible dolor de cabeza *[tairr-eeblay dolor day kabaytha]*

spoke *(in wheel)* el radio *[rad-yo]*

sponge una esponja *[espon-Ha]*

spoon una cuchara

sport el deporte

sport(s) jacket una chaqueta sport

spot: will they do it on the spot? ¿lo harán en el acto? *[lo aran]*; *(on skin)* un grano

sprain: I've sprained my ... me he torcido el ... *[may ay tortheedo]*

spray *(for hair)* una laca

spring *(season)* la primavera *[—baira]*; *(of seat etc)* el muelle *[mway-yay]*

square *(in town)* la plaza *[platha]*; **ten square metres** diez metros cuadrados *[kwadrados]*

squash *(sport)* el squash *[eskw-ash]*

stain *(on clothes)* una mancha

stairs las escaleras

stale pasado

stall: the engine keeps stalling el motor se para a cada rato

stalls butacas de patio *[pat-yo]*

stamp un sello *[se-yo]*; **a stamp for England please** un sello para Inglaterra, por favor

stand: I can't stand … no aguanto … *[agwanto]*

standard (*adjective*) estándar

standby (*fly*) un vuelo standby *[bwaylo]*

star una estrella *[estre-ya]*

start el principio *[preentheep-yo]*; (*verb*) comenzar *[komenthar]*; **when does the film start?** ¿a qué hora comienza la película? *[a kay ora kom-yentha]*; **the car won't start** el coche no arranca

starter (*car*) el motor de arranque *[arrankay]*; (*food*) un entremés

starving: I'm starving me muero de hambre *[may mwairo day ambray]*

state (*in country*) el estado; **the States** (*USA*) los Estados Unidos *[ooneedos]*

station (*for trains*) la estación del ferrocarril *[estath-yon]*

statue la estatua *[estat-wa]*

stay: we enjoyed our stay nos lo hemos pasado muy bien; **where are you staying?** ¿dónde se hospedan? *[ospedan]*; **I'm staying at … hotel** me hospedo en el hotel …; **I'd like to stay another week** me gustaría quedarme otra semana más *[may goostaree-a kay-darmay]*; **I'm staying in tonight** no salgo esta noche

steak un filete *[feelay-tay]*

steal: my bag has been stolen me han robado el bolso *[may an]*

steep (*hill*) empinado

steering (*car*) la dirección *[deerekth-yon]*

steering wheel el volante *[bolantay]*

stereo estéreo

sterling libras esterlinas

stew un estofado

steward (*on plane*) el aereomozo *[a-airo-motho]*

stewardess la azafata *[athafata]*

sticking plaster una tirita

sticky pegajoso *[pega-ноso]*

sticky tape una cinta adhesiva *[theenta ad-eseeba]*

still: I'm still waiting todavía estoy esperando *[todabee-a]*; **will you still be**

open? ¿estarán abiertos todavía?; **it's still not right** todavía no está bien; **that's still better** eso está aún mejor *[a-oon]*

sting: a bee sting una picadura de abeja *[abay-на]*; **I've been stung** algo me ha picado *[algo may a]*

stink un mal olor

stockings las medias *[mayd-yas]*

stolen: my wallet's been stolen me han robado la cartera *[may an]*

stomach el estómago; **do you have something for an upset stomach?** ¿tiene algo para el malestar de estómago? *[t-yenay]*

stomach-ache un dolor de estómago

stone (*rock*) una piedra *[p-yedra]* *see page 118*

stop (*bus stop*) una parada; **which is the stop for …?** ¿cuál es la parada para ir a …? *[kwal]*; **please stop here** (*to taxi-driver*) pare aquí, por favor *[paray akee]*; **do you stop near …?** ¿para cerca de …? *[thairka day]*; **stop doing that!** ¡deje de hacer eso! *[day-нay day athair eso]*

stopover (*airplane*) una escala; (*car, bus, coach*) una parada

store una tienda *[t-yenda]*

storey un piso

storm una tormenta

story un cuento *[kwento]*

stove un horno *[orno]*

straight (*road etc*) derecho; **it's straight ahead** todo derecho; **straight away** en seguida *[seg-eeda]*; **a straight whisky** un whisky solo

straighten: can you straighten things out? ¿puede arreglarlo? *[pway-day]*

strange (*odd*) extraño *[estran-yo]*; (*unknown*) desconocido *[deskonotheedo]*

stranger: I'm a stranger here no soy de aquí *[akee]*

strap la correa *[korray-a]*

strawberry una fresa

streak: could you put streaks in? (*in hair*) ¿puede ponerme unas mechas? *[pway-day ponairmay]*

stream un arroyo

street la calle *[ka-yay]*; **on the street** en la calle

street cafe una terraza *[terratha]*

streetcar un tranvía *[trambee-a]*

streetmap un mapa de la ciudad *[th-*

yooda]
strep throat la garganta inflamada
strike: they're on strike están en huelga
[*welga*]
string una cuerda [*kwairda*]
striped de rayas [*day rye-as*]
striptease un striptease
stroke: he's had a stroke le ha dado un
ataque [*atakay*]
stroll: let's go for a stroll vamos a dar
una vuelta [*bwelta*]
stroller (*for babies*) un cochecito [*kochay-theeto*]
strong (*person, taste, drink*) fuerte
[*fwairtay*]
stroppy (*waiter, official*) pesado
stuck: the key's stuck la llave se ha
atascado [*la yabay say a …*]
student un estudiante [*estood-yante*]
stupid estúpido [*estoo—*]
sty(e) (*in eye*) un orzuelo [*orth-way-lo*]
subtitles los subtítulos [*soobteetoolos*]
suburb el suburbio [*sooboorb-yo*]
subway el metro
successful: was it successful? ¿tuvo
éxito? [*toobo*]
suddenly de repente
sue: I intend to sue voy a poner una
demanda [*boy a ponair*]
suede de ante
sugar el azúcar [*athookar*]
suggest: what do you suggest? ¿qué su-
giere? [*kay soo-ʜyairay*]
suit (*clothes*) un traje [*traʜay*]; **it doesn't
suit me** (*colour etc*) no me sienta bien [*no
may s-yenta b-yen*]; **it suits you** te sienta
muy bien; **that suits me fine** (*plan etc*) me
parece bien [*pa-rethay b-yen*]
suitable conveniente [*komben-yentay*]
suitcase una maleta
sulk: he's sulking está de mal humor
[*oomor*]
sultry (*weather*) húmedo [*oomedo*]
summer el verano [*bairano*]; **in the
summer** en el verano
sun el sol; **in the sun** bajo el sol [*ba-ʜo*];
out of the sun en la sombra; **I've had too
much sun** me ha dado demasiado el sol
sunbathe tomar el sol
sunburn una quemadura del sol [*kayma-doora*]
sunburnt quemado [*kaymado*]
Sunday el domingo

sunglasses gafas de sol
sun lounger (*recliner*) una tumbona
[*toombona*]
sunny: if it's sunny si hace sol [*athay*]
sunrise la salida del sol
sunset la puesta del sol [*pwesta*]
sunshade (*over table*) la sombrilla [*som-breeya*]
sunshine la luz del sol [*looth*]
sunstroke una insolación [*eensolath-yon*]
suntan el bronceado [*bronthay-ado*]
suntan lotion una loción bronceadora
[*lothyon bronthay-adora*]
suntanned bronceado [*bronthay-ado*]
suntan oil el aceite bronceador [*athay-tay*]
sun worshipper un loco por el sol
super (*time, meal etc*) fabuloso; **super!**
¡magnífico!
superb magnífico
supermarket un supermercado [*soo-pairmairkado*]
supper la cena [*thayna*]
supplement (*extra charge*) un suplemento
[*sooplaymento*]
suppose: I suppose so supongo que sí
suppository un supositorio [*sooposeetor-yo*]
sure: I'm sure estoy seguro; **are you
sure?** ¿está seguro?; **he's sure** está seguro; **sure!** ¡por supuesto! [*soopwesto*]
surf el surf
surfing: to go surfing hacer surfing
[*athair*]
surfboard un tabla de surf
surname el apellido [*ap-eyeedo*]
surprise una sorpresa
surprising: that's not surprising no me
sorprende [*no may*]
suspension (*on car*) la suspensión [*soos-pens-yon*]
swallow (*verb*) tragar
swearword una palabrota
sweat (*verb*) sudar [*soodar*]; **covered in
sweat** empapado en sudor [*soodor*]
sweater un suéter
Sweden Suecia [*swayth-ya*]
sweet dulce [*doolthay*]; (*dessert*) el postre
sweets los caramelos
swelling una hinchazón [*eenchathon*]
sweltering: it's sweltering hace un calor
sofocante [*athay*]
swerve: I had to swerve tuve que girar

repentinamente *[toobay kay неerar]*
swim: I'm going for a swim voy a nadar
[boy]; **do you want to go for a swim?**
¿quieres ir a nadar? *[k-yairays]*; **I can't
swim** no sé nadar *[no say]*
swimming la natación *[natath-yon]*; **I
like swimming** me gusta la natación
swimming costume un traje de baño
[tra-нay day banyo]
swimming pool una piscina *[pees-
theena]*
swimming trunks un traje de baño

[tra-нay day banyo]
switch el interruptor *[eentairrooptor]*;
could you switch it on? ¿lo puede
encender? *[pway-day enthendair]*;
could you switch it off? ¿lo puede
apagar? *[pway-day]*
Switzerland Suiza *[soo-eetha]*
swollen inflamado
swollen glands las glándulas inflamadas
[glandoolas]
synagogue una sinagoga
synthetic sintético

T

table una mesa *[may-sa]*; **a table for two**
una mesa para dos; **at our usual table** en
nuestra mesa de costumbre *[kostoom-
bray]*
tablecloth un mantel
table d'hote el menú del día *[menoo]*
table tennis el ping-pong *[peeng]*
table wine el vino de mesa *[beeno day
may-sa]*
tactful diplomático
tailback una caravana de coches *[karaba-
na]*
tailor un sastre
take coger *[koнair]*; **will you take this to
room 12?** ¿podría llevar esto a la habitación número doce? *[podree-a yaybar]*;
will you take me to Hotel ...? ¿podría
llevarme al Hotel ...?; **do you take credit
cards?** ¿acepta tarjetas de crédito?
[athepta tar-нaytas]; **ok, I'll take it** está
bien, lo compro; **how long does it take
to get to Madrid?** ¿cuánto se tarda en ir a
Madrid? *[kwanto]*; **it took 2 hours** tardó
dos horas; **is this seat taken?** ¿está
ocupado este asiento? *[as-yento]*; **I can't
take too much sun** no puedo tomar el sol
mucho tiempo *[no pway-do]*; **a
hamburger to take away** una hamburguesa para llevar *[amboorgaysa para
yay-bar]*; **will you take this back, it's
broken** quiero devolver esto, está roto

[k-yairo daybolbair]; **could you take it
in at the side?** *(dress)* ¿podría metérmelo
de este lado? *[podree-a metairmaylo]*;
when does the plane take off? ¿a qué
hora sale el avión? *[salay el ab-yon]*; **can
you take a little off the top?** córteme un
poco de arriba *[kortay-may]*
talcum powder el talco
talk hablar *[ablar]*
tall alto
tampax *(tm)* un tampax
tampons los tampones
tan un bronceado *[bronthay-ado]*; **I want
to get a good tan** quiero ponerme muy
moreno *[k-yairo ponairmay]*
tank *(of car)* el depósito
tap el grifo
tape *(for cassette)* una cinta *[theenta]*;
(sticky) una cinta adhesiva *[ad-eseeba]*
tape measure una cinta métrica
[theenta]
tape recorder un magnetofón
taste el sabor; **can I taste it?** ¿puedo pro-
barlo? *[pway-do]*; **it has a peculiar taste**
tiene un sabor raro *[ra-ro]*; **it tastes very
nice** sabe muy bien *[sabay mwee b-yen]*;
it tastes revolting sabe muy mal
taxi un taxi; **will you get me a taxi?**
¿podría conseguirme un taxi *[podree-a
konseg-eermay]*
taxi-driver el taxista

taxi rank la parada de taxis
tea (*drink*) un té *[tay]*; **tea for two please** dos tés, por favor; **could I have a cup of tea?** un té, por favor
teabag una bolsa de té
teach: could you teach me? ¿podría enseñarme? *[podree-a ensen-yarmay]*; **could you teach me Spanish?** ¿podría enseñarme español? *[espan-yol]*
teacher (*junior*) el maestro *[my-estro]*; (*secondary*) el profesor
team el equipo *[ekeepo]*
teapot la tetera *[tetaira]*
tea towel un paño de cocina *[kotheena]*
teenager un adolescente *[adolesthentay]*
teetotal abstemio
telegram un telegrama; **I want to send a telegram** quiero mandar un telegrama *[k-yairo]*
telephone el teléfono; **can I make a telephone call?** ¿puedo llamar por teléfono? *[pway-do yamar]*; **could you talk to him for me on the telephone?** ¿podría hablar por teléfono con él de mi parte? *[podree-a ablar]*
telephone box una cabina telefónica
telephone directory la guía telefónica *[g-ee-a]*
telephone number el número de teléfono *[noomairo]*; **what's your telephone number?** ¿cuál es su número de teléfono? *[kwal]*
telephoto lens un teleobjetivo *[telay-opнeteebo]*
television la televisión *[telaybees-yon]*; **I'd like to watch television** quisiera ver televisión *[kees-yaira bair]*; **is the match on television?** ¿van a televisar el partido? *[ban a telebeesar]*
tell: could you tell him ...? ¿podría decirle ...? *[podree-a detheerlay]*; **I can't tell the difference** no veo ninguna diferencia *[no bay-o neengoona deefairenth-ya]*
temperature (*weather etc*) la temperatura *[tempairatoora]*; **he has a temperature** tiene fiebre *[t-yenay f-yaybray]*
temporary temporal
tenant (*of apartment*) un inquilino *[eenkeeleeno]*
tennis el tenis
tennis ball una pelota de tenis
tennis court una pista de tenis; **can we use the tennis court?** ¿podemos usar la pista de tenis? *[podaymos oosar]*
tennis racket una raqueta de tenis *[rakay-ta]*
tent una tienda de campaña *[t-yenda day kampan-ya]*
term (*school*) el trimestre
terminus la estación terminal *[estath-yon tairmeenal]*
terrace la terraza *[tairratha]*; **on the terrace** en la terraza
terrible terrible *[tairreeblay]*
terrific fabuloso *[fabooloso]*
testicle un testículo
than que *[kay]*; **smaller than** más pequeño que
thanks, thank you gracias *[grath-yas]*; **thank you very much** muchas gracias; **thank you for everything** gracias por todo; **no thanks** no, gracias
that: that woman esa mujer *[moo-нair]*; **that man** ese hombre *[ombray]*; **that one** ése; **I hope that ...** espero que ... *[espairo]*; **that's not ...** eso no es ...; **that's perfect** es perfecto *[pairfekto]*; **that's very strange** es muy raro; **that's it** (*that's right*) eso es; **is it that expensive?** ¿tan caro es?
the (*singular*) el; la (*plural*) los; las *see page 100*
theater, theatre el teatro *[tay-atro]*
their su; sus *[soo; soos] see page 103*
theirs su, sus; suyos, suyas; de ellos, de ellas *see page 107*
them (*objects*) los; las; (*persons*) les *[lays]*; **for them** para ellos *[eyos] see page 105*
then entonces *[enton-thays]*
there allí *[a-yee]*; **over there** allí *[a-yee]*; **up there** allí arriba *[a-yee]*; **is/are there ...?** ¿hay ...? *[eye]*; **there you are** (*giving something*) aquí tiene *[akee t-yenay]*
thermal spring una fuente termal *[fwentay tairmal]*
thermometer un termómetro *[tairmo-metro]*
thermos flask un termo *[tairmo]*
thermostat el termostato *[tairmostato]*
these éstos; éstas; **can I have these?** ¿me puedo llevar éstos? *[may pway-do yaybar]*
they ellos; ellas *[eyos, eyas]*; **are they ready?** ¿están listos?; **are they coming?** ¿van a venir? *[ban a beneer] see page 105*

thick grueso *[grwayso]*; (*stupid*) estúpido *[estoopeedo]*

thief un ladrón

thigh el muslo *[mooslo]*

thin (*material, person*) delgado

thing una cosa; **have you seen my things?** ¿ha visto mis cosas? *[a beesto]*; **first thing in the morning** a primera hora de la mañana *[a preemaira ora]*

think pensar; **what do you think?** ¿qué piensa? *[kay p-yensa]*; **I think so** creo que sí *[kray-o kay see]*; **I don't think so** no lo creo *[no lo kray-o]*; **I'll think about it** lo pensaré *[lo pensaray]*

third-class (*travel*) en tercera clase *[tairthaira]*

third party (*insurance*) un seguro contra tercera persona *[segooro kontra tairthaira pairsona]*

thirsty: I'm thirsty tengo sed

this: this hotel este hotel *[otel]*; **this street** esta calle *[ka-yay]*; **this one** éste; ésta; **this is my wife** (*introduction*) le presento a mi mujer *[… mee moo-наir …]*; **this is my favo(u)rite cafe** es mi café favorito *[faboreeto]*; **is this yours?** ¿es suyo?, ¿es de usted?; **this is …** (*on phone*) habla … *[abla]*

those esos; esas; **not these, those** no éstos, ésos

thread un hilo *[eelo]*

throat la garganta

throat lozenges unas pastillas para la garganta *[pastee-yas]*

throttle (*motorbike, boat*) el acelerador *[athelairador]*

through a través de *[a trabess day]*; **does it go through Pamplona?** ¿va a Pamplona? *[ba]*; **Monday through Friday** de lunes a viernes; **straight through the city centre** a través del centro de la ciudad *[thentro day la th-yooda]*

through train un tren directo

throw tirar; **don't throw it away** no lo tire *[teeray]*; **I'm going to throw up** voy a vomitar *[boy a bomeetar]*

thumb el dedo pulgar *[poolgar]*

thumbtack un chinche *[cheenchay]*

thunder un trueno *[trway-no]*

thunderstorm una tormenta eléctrica

Thursday el jueves *[нwaybays]*

ticket un billete *[beeyay-tay]*; (*cinema*) una entrada; (*cloakroom, checkroom*) un ticket *[tee-kay]*

ticket office la taquilla *[takee-ya]*

tide: at low tide cuando la marea está baja *[kwando la maray-a esta ba-на]*; **at high tide** cuando la marea está alta

tie (*necktie*) una corbata

tight (*clothes*) ajustado *[aноostado]*; **the waist is too tight** está muy ajustado en la cintura *[theentoora]*

tights unos panties

time el tiempo *[t-yempo]*; **what's the time?** ¿qué hora es? *[kay ora ess]*; **at what time do you close?** ¿a qué hora cierran? *[th-yairran]*; **there's not much time** no hay mucho tiempo *[no eye]*; **for the time being** por el momento; **from time to time** de vez en cuando *[day beth en kwando]*; **right on time** justo a tiempo *[ноosto a t-yempo]*; **this time** esta vez *[beth]*; **last time** la última vez *[oolteema beth]*; **next time** la próxima vez; **four times** cuatro veces *[kwatro bethays]*; **have a good time!** ¡que se divierta! *[kay say deeb-yairta] see page 116*

timetable el horario *[orar-yo]*

tin (*can*) una lata

tinfoil un papel de aluminio

tin-opener un abrelatas

tint (*hair*) teñir *[ten-yeer]*

tiny diminuto *[deemeenooto]*

tip una propina; **does that include the tip?** ¿está incluida la propina? *[esta eenklweeda]*

tire una rueda *[rwayda]*

tired cansado; **I'm tired** estoy cansado

tiring agotador

tissues kleenex (*tm*)

to: to Madrid/England a Madrid/Inglaterra *[ah madree]*; **to the airport** al aeropuerto *[a-airo-pwairto]*; **here's to you!** (*toast*) ¡a tu salud! *[saloo] see page 116*

toast una tostada; (*drinking*) un brindis *[breendees]*

tobacco el tabaco

tobacconist, tobacco store el estanco

today hoy *[oy]*

today week de hoy en una semana

toe un dedo del pie *[p-yay]*

toffee un toffee *[tofay]*

together junto *[ноonto]*; **we're together** venimos juntos *[beneemos]*; **can we pay together?** ¿nos trae una sola cuenta, por favor? *[nos tra-ay oona sola kwenta]*

toilet los servicios *[sairbeeth-yos]*; **where's the toilet?** ¿dónde están los servicios?; **I want to go to the toilet** quiero ir al servicio *[k-yairo]*; **she's in the toilet** ha ido al cuarto de baño *[a eedo al kwarto day banyo]*

toilet paper el papel higiénico *[eeнyen-eeko]*

toilet water una colonia

toll el peaje *[pay-aнay]*; **motorway toll** el peaje

tomato un tomate *[tomatay]*

tomato juice un zumo de tomate *[thoomo day tomatay]*

tomato ketchup la salsa de tomate *[tomatay]*

tomorrow mañana *[man-yana]*; **tomorrow morning** mañana por la mañana; **tomorrow afternoon** mañana por la tarde; **tomorrow evening** mañana por la noche *[notchay]*; **the day after tomorrow** pasado mañana; **see you tomorrow** hasta mañana *[asta]*

ton una tonelada *see page 118*

tongue la lengua *[leng-gwa]*

tonic (*water*) una tónica

tonight esta noche *[notchay]*; **not tonight** esta noche no

tonsillitis las anginas *[an-нeenas]*

tonsils las anginas *[an-нeenas]*

too demasiado *[demass-yado]*; (*also*) también *[tamb-yen]*; **too much** demasiado; **me too** yo también; **I'm not feeling too good** no me siento muy bien *[no may s-yento mwee b-yen]*

tool una herramienta *[airram-yenta]*

tooth un diente *[d-yentay]*; (*back tooth*) una muela *[mwayla]*

toothache dolor de muelas *[mwaylas]*

toothbrush un cepillo de dientes *[theepeeyo day d-yentays]*

toothpaste una pasta de dientes *[d-yentays]*

top: on top of ... encima de *[entheema day]*; **on top of the car** encima del coche; **on the top floor** en el último piso *[... oolteemo ...]*; **at the top** en lo alto; **at the top of the hill** en la cima de la colina *[... theema ...]*; **top quality** de alta calidad *[kaleeda]*; **bikini top** la parte de arriba del bikini

topless topless; **topless beach** una playa nudista *[ply-a noo—]*

torch una linterna *[leentairna]*

total el total

touch tocar; **let's keep in touch** ¡a ver si mantenemos el contacto! *[a bair see]*

tough (*meat*) dura *[doora]*; **tough luck!** ¡mala suerte! *[swairtay]*

tour un viaje *[b-yaнay]*; **is there a tour of ...?** ¿hay una gira por ...? *[eye oona нeera]*

tour guide el guía turístico *[g-ee-a]*

tourist un turista *[tooreesta]*

tourist office la oficina de turismo *[ofeetheena]*

touristy: somewhere not so touristy un sitio en que no haya muchos turistas *[oon seet-yo en kay no eye-a]*

tour operator la agencia de viajes *[aнenth-ya day b-yaнays]*

tow: can you give me a tow? ¿puede remolcarme? *[pway-day]*

toward(s) hacia *[ath-ya]*; **toward(s) Salamanca** hacia Salamanca

towel una toalla *[to-aya]*

town una ciudad *[th-yooda]*; (*smaller*) un pueblo *[pweblo]*; **in town** en el centro *[thentro]*; **which bus goes into town?** ¿qué autobús va al centro? *[kay owtoboos ba]*; **we're staying just out of town** vivimos en las afueras de la ciudad *[beebeemos en las afwairas day la th-yooda]*

town hall el ayuntamiento *[ayoonta—]*

tow rope un cable de remolque *[kablay day remolkay]*

toy un juguete *[нoogay-tay]*

track suit un chándal

traditional tradicional *[tradeeth-yonal]*; **a traditional Spanish meal** una comida típica española

traffic: el tráfico

traffic circle una glorieta *[glor-yayta]*

traffic cop el guardia de tráfico *[gward-ya]*

traffic jam un embotellamiento *[emboteyam-yento]*

traffic light(s) los semáforos

trailer (*for carrying tent etc*) un remolque *[remolkay]*; (*caravan*) una caravana *[—abana]*

train el tren; **when's the next train to ...?** ¿a qué hora sale el próximo tren para ...? *[a kay ora salay]*; **by train** en tren

trainers (*shoes*) unas playeras *[ply-airas]*

train station la estación del ferrocarril

[estath-yon]

tram un tranvía *[trambee-a]*

tramp (*person*) un vagabundo *[baga-boondo]*

tranquillizers unos calmantes

transatlantic transatlántico

transformer un transformador

transistor (*radio*) una radio

translate traducir *[—ootheer]*; **could you translate that?** ¿podría traducir eso? *[podree-a]*

translation una traducción *[tradookth-yon]*

transit desk el mostrador de tránsito

transmission (*of car*) la transmisión *[transmeess-yon]*

travel viajar *[b-yaнar]*; **we're travel(l)ing around** estamos viajando *[b-yaнando]*

travel agent un agente de viajes *[aнentay day b-yaнays]*

travel(l)er un viajero *[b-yaнairo]*

traveller's cheque, traveler's check un cheque de viaje *[chekay day b-yaнay]*

tray una bandeja *[banday-нa]*

tree un árbol

tremendous tremendo

trendy (*bar, clothes, person*) moderno *[modairno]*

tricky (*difficult*) complicado

trim: just a trim please córtemelo sólo un poco, por favor *[kortaymaylo]*

trip una excursión *[esskoors-yon]*; **I'd like to go on a trip to ...** me gustaría hacer una excursión a ... *[may goostaree-a athair]*; **have a good trip** ¡buen viaje! *[bwen b-yaнay]*

tripod un trípode *[treepoday]*

tropical tropical

trouble problemas; **I'm having trouble with ...** tengo problemas con ...; **sorry to trouble you** perdone que le moleste

trousers los pantalones

trouser suit un traje pantalón *[traнay]*

trout una trucha *[troocha]*

truck un camión *[kam-yon]*

truck driver un camionero *[kamyonairo]*

true verdadero *[bair-dadairo]*; **that's not true** no es verdad *[bairda]*

trunk (*of car*) el portaequipajes *[porta-ekeepaнays]*

trunks (*swimming*) un traje de baño *[traнay day banyo]*

truth la verdad *[bairda]*; **it's the truth** es la verdad

try intentar; **please try** haga el favor de intentarlo *[aga el fabor]*; **I've never tried it** no lo he probado nunca *[no lo ay]*; **can I have a try?** ¿puedo probar? *[pway-do]*; **may I try it on?** ¿puedo probármelo? *[pway-do]*

T-shirt una camiseta

tube (*for car tyre*) la cámara de aire *[eye-ray]*

Tuesday el martes

tuition: I'd like tuition quiero recibir clases *[k-yairo retheebeer]*

tulip un tulipán *[too—]*

tuna fish el atún *[atoon]*

tune una melodía

Tunisia Túnez *[tooneth]*

tunnel un túnel *[toonell]*

Turkey Turquía *[toorkee-a]*

turn: it's my turn next el próximo es mi turno *[mee toorno]*; **turn left** gire a la izquierda *[нeeray a la eethk-yairda]*; **where do we turn off?** ¿dónde tenemos que desviarnos? *[donday tenaymos kay dezb-yarnos]*; **can you turn the air-conditioning on?** ¿podría encender el aire acondicionado? *[podree-a enthendair el eye-ray akondeeth-yona-do]*; **can you turn the air-conditioning off?** ¿podría apagar el aire acondicionado? *[podree-a apagar el eye-ray akondeeth-yonado]*; **he didn't turn up** no vino *[no beeno]*

turning: at the next turning en el próximo desvío *[dezbee-o]*

TV la tele

tweezers unas pinzas *[peenthas]*

twice dos veces *[bethays]*; **twice as much** el doble *[doblay]*

twin beds las camas gemelas *[нay-maylas]*

twins unos gemelos *[нay-maylos]*

twist: I've twisted my ankle me he torcido el tobillo *[may ay tortheedo el tobee-yo]*

type un tipo; **a different type of ...** un tipo diferente de ...

typewriter una máquina de escribir *[makeena]*

typhoid el tifus *[teefoos]*

typical típico

tyre una rueda *[rwayda]*

U

ugly feo
ulcer una úlcera *[oolthaira]*
Ulster Ulster *[oolstair]*
umbrella un paraguas *[paragwas]*
uncle: my uncle mi tío
uncomfortable incómodo
unconscious inconsciente *[eenkonsthyentay]*
under debajo de *[deba-но day]*
underdone (*food*) demasiado poco hecho *[day-mas-yado poko aycho]*
underground (*railway*) el metro
underpants los calzoncillos *[kalthontheeyos]*
undershirt una camiseta
understand: I don't understand no entiendo *[no ent-yendo]*; **I understand** lo entiendo; **do you understand?** ¿entiende usted? *[ent-yenday oostay]*
underwear la ropa interior
undo (*clothes*) desatar
uneatable: it's uneatable no hay quien lo coma *[no eye k-yen]*
unemployed en paro
unfair: that's unfair es injusto *[eenноosto]*
unfortunately desafortunadamente
unfriendly antipático
unhappy infeliz *[eenfeleeth]*
unhealthy (*food, climate, lifestyle*) malsano
United States los Estados Unidos *[oo—]*; **in the United States** en Estados Unidos
university la universidad *[ooneebairseeda]*
unlimited mileage sin límite de kilometraje *[seen leemeetay day keelometraнay]*
unlock abrir; **the door was unlocked** la puerta no estaba cerrada con llave *[thairrada kon yabay]*
unpack deshacer las maletas *[desathair]*
unpleasant desagradable *[—ablay]*
untie desatar
until hasta que *[asta kay]*; **until we meet again** hasta la próxima; **not until next Wednesday** no hasta el próximo miércoles
unusual poco común *[komoon]*
up arriba; **further up the road** más adelante; **up there** allí arriba *[ayee]*; **he's not up yet** todavía no se ha levantado *[todabee-a no say a lebantado]*; **what's up?** ¿qué pasa? *[kay]*
upmarket (*restaurant, bar*) de lujo *[day looно]*
upset stomach malestar de estómago *[mal-estar]*
upside down al revés *[rebess]*
upstairs arriba
urgent urgente *[oorнentay]*; **it's very urgent** es muy urgente *[mwee]*
urinary tract infection una infección en las vías urinarias *[infekth-yon en las bee-as ooreenar-yas]*
us: please help us ayúdenos, por favor *[ayooday-nos]*; **with us** con nosotros; **for us** para nosotros *see page 105*
use: may I use …? ¿podría usar …? *[podree-a oosar]*
used: I used to swim a lot solía nadar bastante; **when I get used to the heat** cuando me acostumbre al calor *[kwando may akostoombray]*
useful útil *[ooteel]*
usual habitual *[abeetwal]*; **as usual** como de costumbre *[day kostoombray]*
usually normalmente
U-turn un cambio de sentido

V

vacancy: do you have any vacancies?
(*hotel*) ¿tiene habitaciones libres? *[t-yenay abeetath-yonays leebrays]*
vacation las vacaciones *[bakath-yonays]*; **we're here on vacation** estamos de vacaciones
vaccination una vacuna *[bakoona]*
vacuum cleaner la aspiradora
vacuum flask un termo *[tairmo]*
vagina la vagina *[baнeena]*
valid válido *[baleedo]*; **how long is it valid for?** ¿hasta cuándo tiene validez? *[asta kwando t-yenay baleedeth]*
valley un valle *[ba-yay]*
valuable valioso *[bal-yoso]*; **can I leave my valuables here?** ¿puedo dejar aquí mis objetos de valor? *[pway-do deнar akee mees ob-нaytos day balor]*
value valor *[balor]*
van una furgoneta *[foo—]*
vanilla vainilla *[by-neeya]*; **vanilla ice cream** un helado de vainilla *[elado]*
varicose veins las varices *[bareethays]*
variety show un espectáculo de variedades *[bar-yaydadays]*
vary: it varies depende
vase el florero
vaudeville (*variety*) un espectáculo de variedades *[bar-yaydadays]*
VD una enfermedad venérea *[enfairmayda benairay-a]*
veal ternera *[tairnaira]*
vegetables unas verduras *[bairdooras]*
vegetarian un vegetariano *[beнetar-yano]*; **I'm a vegetarian** soy vegetariano
velvet el terciopelo *[tairth-yopaylo]*
vending machine (*for cigarettes etc*) una máquina de ... *[makeena]*

ventilator el ventilador *[ben—]*
verruca hongos *[ongos]*
very muy *[mwee]*; **just a very little Spanish** sólo un poquito de castellano *[pookeeto day kas-teyano]*; **just a very little for me** sólo un poquito para mí; **I like it very much** me gusta mucho *[may goosta moocho]*
vest (*undershirt*) una camiseta; (*waistcoat*) un chaleco
via por; **via San Sebastian** por San Sebastián
video un video *[beeday-o]*
view la vista *[beesta]*; **what a superb view!** ¡qué vista tan fabulosa!
viewfinder el visor *[beesor]*
villa un chalet
village un pueblo *[pweblo]*
vine una vid *[beeth]*
vinegar el vinagre *[beenagray]*
vine-growing area una zona de vinos *[thona day beenos]*
vineyard un viñedo *[been-yaydo]*
vintage la cosecha; **vintage wine** un vino añejo *[beeno an-yayнo]*
visa un visado *[beesado]*
visibility visibilidad *[bee—]*
visit visitar *[beeseetar]*; **I'd like to visit ...** me gustaría ir a ...; **come and visit us** ven a visitarnos *[ben a bee—]*
vital: it's vital that ... es de vital importancia que ... *[es day beetal eemportanth-ya kay]*
vitamins las vitaminas *[bee—]*
vodka un vodka *[bodka]*
voice una voz *[both]*
voltage el voltaje *[bolta-нay]*
vomit vomitar *[bo—]*

W X Y Z

wafer (*ice cream*) un helado de corte *[elado]*

waist la cintura *[theentoora]*

waistcoat el chaleco

wait esperar *[espairar]*; **wait for me** espéreme *[espay-ray-may]*; **don't wait for me** no me espere(n); **it was worth waiting for** valió la pena haber esperado *[bal-yo]*; **I'll wait till my wife comes** esperaré a que venga mi mujer *[benga mee mooнair]*; **I'll wait a little longer** esperaré un rato más; **can you do it while I wait?** ¿puede hacerlo mientras espero? *[pway-day athairlo m-yentras]*

waiter un camarero; **waiter!** ¡camarero!

waiting room (*at station*) la sala de espera

waitress una camarera; **waitress!** ¡señorita! *[sen-yoreeta]*

wake: will you wake me up at 6.30? ¿podría despertarme a las seis y media? *[podree-a]*

Wales Gales *[galays]*

walk: let's walk there vamos a pie *[bamos a p-yay]*; **is it possible to walk there?** ¿se puede ir a pie? *[say pway-day]*; **I'll walk back** volveré a pie *[bolbairay]*; **is it a long walk?** ¿es una caminata larga?; **it's only a short walk** está cerca *[thairka]*; **I'm going out for a walk** voy a dar una vuelta *[boy a dar oona bwelta]*; **let's take a walk around town** vamos a dar un paseo por la ciudad *[bamos a dar oom pasay-o por la th-yooda]*

walking: I want to do some walking quiero andar un poco *[k-yairo]*

walking boots las botas de montañismo

walking stick un bastón

walkman (*tm*) un cassette individual *[eendeebeed-wal]*

wall (*inside*) la pared; (*garden etc*) la tapia

wallet la billetera *[beeyay-taira]*

wander: I like just wandering around me gusta pasear

want: I want a ... quiero un/una ... *[k-yairo]*; **I don't want any ...** no quiero ninguno(a); **I want to go home** quiero

irme a casa *[k-yairo eermay]*; **but I want to** pero yo quiero; **I don't want to** no quiero; **he wants to ...** quiere ... *[k-yairay]*; **what do you want?** ¿qué quiere? *[kay k-yairay]*

war la guerra *[gerra]*

ward (*in hospital*) una sala

warm caliente *[kal-yentay]*; **it's so warm today** ¡qué calor hace hoy! *[kay kalor athay oy]*; **I'm so warm** ¡tengo tanto calor!

warning una advertencia *[adbairtenth-ya]*

was it was ... era, estaba *[aira ...]* see page 110

wash lavar *[labar]*; **I need a wash** necesito lavarme *[netheseeto labarmay]*; **can you wash the car?** ¿puede lavar el coche? *[pway-day]*; **can you wash these?** ¿puede lavarlos *[pway-day]*; **it'll wash off** (*stain etc*) saldrá al lavarlo

washcloth (*face cloth*) un guante de baño *[gwantay day banyo]*

washer (*for bolt etc*) una arandela

washhand basin un lavabo *[lababo]*

washing: where can I hang my washing? ¿dónde puedo tender la ropa? *[... pwaydo ...]*; **can you do my washing for me?** ¿puede lavarme la ropa? *[pway-day]*

washing machine una lavadora *[lab—]*

washing powder el jabón en polvo *[нabon em polbo]*

washing-up: I'll do the washing-up yo lavaré los platos *[labaray]*

washing-up liquid el detergente lavavajíllas *[daytair-нentay lababaнeeyas]*

wasp una avispa *[abeespa]*

wasteful: that's wasteful es un desperdicio *[despairdeeth-yo]*

wastepaper basket una papelera

watch (*wrist-*) el reloj *[reloн]*; **will you watch my things for me?** ¿puede cuidarme mis cosas? *[pway-day kweedarmay]*; **I'll just watch** miraré so-

lamente; **watch out!** ¡cuidado!
[kweedado]
watch strap la correa del reloj *[korray-a]*
water el agua *[agwa]*; **may I have some
water?** ¿me da un poco de agua?
watercolour (*painting*) una acuarela
[akwarela]
waterproof impermeable *[eempairmay-
ablay]*
waterski: I'd like to learn to waterski
me gustaría aprender a hacer esquí acuático *[athair eskee akwateeko]*
waterskiing el esquí acuático *[eskee
akwateeko]*
water sports los deportes acuáticos
[akwateekos]
water wings unos manguitos *[man-
geetos]*
wave (*sea*) una ola
way: which way is it? ¿por dónde? *[por
donday]*; **it's this way** es por aquí
[akee]; **it's that way** es por allí *[ayee]*;
could you tell me the way to ...? ¿podría indicarme el camino a ...? *[podree-a
eendeekarmay]*; **is it on the way to
Barcelona?** ¿queda en el camino a
Barcelona? *[kayda]*; **you're blocking
the way** (*with parked car etc*) está obstru-
yendo la vía *[... opstrooyendo la bee-a]*;
is it a long way to ...? ¿queda lejos ...?
[kayda lay*nos]*; **would you show me
the way to do it?** ¿podría mostrarme
cómo hacerlo? *[podree-a mostrarmay
komo athairlo]*; **do it this way** hágalo de
esta manera *[agalo]*; **we want to eat the
Spanish way** queremos comer como los
españoles; **no way!** ¡de ninguna manera!
we nosotros; **we're English/American**
somos ingleses/americanos; **we're
leaving tomorrow** nos vamos mañana
[bamos] see page 105
weak (*person*) débil
wealthy rico
weather el tiempo *[t-yempo]*; **what foul
weather!** ¡qué tiempo tan malo!; **what
beautiful weather!** ¡qué tiempo tan
bueno! *[bweno]*
weather forecast el pronóstico del
tiempo *[t-yempo]*
wedding una boda
wedding anniversary el aniversario de
bodas *[aneebairsar-yo]*
wedding ring el anillo de boda *[aneeyo]*

Wednesday el miércoles *[m-yairkolays]*
week una semana; **a week (from) today**
dentro de una semana; **a week (from)
tomorrow** de mañana en ocho días;
Monday week este lunes no, el otro
weekend: at/on the weekend el fin de
semana
weight el peso; **I want to lose weight**
quiero adelgazar *[k-yairo ad-elgathar]*
weight limit el límite de peso
weird (*thing to happen, person, taste*) raro
welcome: welcome to ... bienvenido(s) a
...; **you're welcome** de nada
well: I don't feel well no me siento bien
[no may s-yento b-yen]; **I haven't been
very well** no he estado bien; **she's not
well** no se siente bien *[no say s-yentay
b-yen]*; **how are you? — very well,
thanks** ¿cómo está? — muy bien, gracias
[... mwee b-yen grath-yas]; **you speak
English very well** habla inglés muy bien
[abla eenglays mwee b-yen]; **me as well**
yo también; **well done!** ¡bravo! *[brabo]*;
well, ... bueno, ... *[bweno]*; **well well!**
¡pero bueno!
well-done (*steak*) muy hecho *[mwee ay-
cho]*
wellingtons unas botas de agua *[agwa]*
Welsh galés *[galays]*
were *see page 110*
west el oeste *[o-estay]*; **to the west** al oeste
West Indian antillano *[anteeyano]*
West Indies las Antillas *[anteeyas]*
wet mojado *[monado]*; **it's all wet** está
todo mojado; **it's been wet all week** ha
llovido toda la semana *[a yobeedo]*
wet suit un traje isotérmico *[tra-nay
eessotair-meeko]*
what? ¿qué? *[kay]*; **what's that?** ¿qué es
eso?; **what are you drinking?** (*can I get
you one*) ¿quiere algo de beber? *[k-yairay]*;
I don't know what to do no sé que hacer
[no say kay athair]; **what a view!** ¡qué
vista! *[beesta]*
wheel la rueda *[r-wayda]*
wheelchair la silla de ruedas *[seeya day
r-waydas]*
when? ¿cuándo? *[kwando]*; **when we get
back** cuando volvamos *[bolbamos]*
where? ¿dónde? *[donday]*; **where is ...?**
¿dónde está ...?; **I don't know where he
is** no sé dónde está; **that's where I left it**
yo lo dejé allí *[day-nay ayee]*

which: **which bus?** ¿qué autobús? *[kay]*;
which one? ¿cuál? *[kwal]*; **which is
yours?** ¿cuál es el suyo?; **I forget
which it was** no recuerdo cuál era *[no
rekwairdo]*; **the one which ...** el que ...
while: **while I'm here** mientras esté aquí
[m-yentras estay akee]
whipped cream la nata batida
whisky un whisky
whisper cuchichear *[koocheechay-ar]*
white blanco
white wine el vino blanco *[beeno]*
Whitsun Pentecostés
who? ¿quién? *[k-yen]*; **who was that?**
¿quién era?; **the man who ...** el hombre
que ... *[ombray kay]*
whole: **the whole week** toda la semana;
two whole days dos días enteros; **the
whole lot** todo
whooping cough la tosferina
whose: **whose is this?** ¿de quién es esto?
[day k-yen]
why? ¿por qué? *[por kay]*; **why not?** ¿por
qué no?; **that's why it's not working** es
por eso que no funciona *[foonth-yona]*
wide ancho
wide-angle lens un lente granangular
widow la viuda *[b-yooda]*
widower el viudo *[b-yoodo]*
wife: **my wife** mi mujer *[mee moo-nair]*
wig una peluca *[pelooka]*
will: **will you ...?** ¿puede ...? *[pway-day]*
see page 112
win ganar; **who won?** ¿quién ha ganado?
[k-yen a]
wind el viento *[b-yento]*
windmill un molino de viento *[b-yento]*
window la ventana *[ben—]*; *(of shop)* el
escaparate *[—atay]*; **near the window**
cerca de la ventana *[thairka]*; **in the
window** *(of shop)* en el escaparate
window seat el asiento junto a la ventana
[as-yento noonto a la bentana]
windscreen, windshield el parabrisas
**windscreen wipers, windshield wip-
ers** los limpiaparabrisas *[leemp-ya—]*
windsurf: **I'd like to windsurf** me gustaría hacer windsurf *[may goostaree-a
athair]*
windsurfing el windsurf
windy: **it's so windy** hace mucho viento
[athay moocho b-yento]
wine el vino *[beeno]*; **can we have some**

more wine? ¿podría traernos más vino?
[podree-a tra-airnos]
wine glass un vaso de vino *[baso day
beeno]*
wine list la lista de vinos *[beenos]*
wine-tasting la catación de vinos *[katath-
yon day beenos]*
wing el ala
wing mirror el espejo retrovisor exterior
[espay-ho retrobeesor estair-yor]
winter el invierno *[eemb-yairno]*; **in the
winter** en el invierno
winter holiday las vacaciones de invierno
[bakath-yonays day eemb-yairno]
winter sports los deportes de invierno
[eemb-yairno]
wire un alambre; *(elec)* un cable eléctrico
[kablay]
wireless una radio *[rad-yo]*
wiring *(in house)* la instalación eléctrica
[eenstalath-yon]
wish: **wishing you were here** ¡me gustaría que estuvieras aquí! *[may goostaree-a
kay estoob-yairas akee]*; **best wishes** sa-
ludos
with con; **I'm staying with ...** estoy en
casa de ...
without sin *[seen]*
witness un testigo; **will you be a witness
for me?** ¿acepta ser mi testigo? *[athepta]*
witty *(person)* ingenioso *[een-Hen-yoso]*
wobble: **it wobbles** *(wheel etc)* se tambalea
[tambalay-a]
woman una mujer *[moo-Hair]*; **women**
las mujeres *[moo-Hairays]*
wonderful estupendo *[—too—]*
won't: **it won't start** no arranca *see page
112*
wood *(material)* la madera
woods *(forest)* el bosque *[boskay]*
wool la lana
word una palabra; **what does that word
mean?** ¿qué significa esa palabra?; **you
have my word** te lo prometo
work trabajar *[trabaHar]*; **how does it
work?** ¿cómo funciona? *[foonth-yona]*;
it's not working no funciona *[foonth-
yona]*; **I work in an office** trabajo en
una oficina *[trabaHo]*; **do you have any
work for me?** ¿tiene trabajo para mí?
[t-yenay]; **when do you finish work?** ¿a
qué hora sale del trabajo? *[a kay ora]*
world el mundo

worn-out (*person*) agotado; (*clothes, shoes*) gastado

worry: I'm worried about her me tiene preocupado [*may t-yenay pray-okoopado*]; **don't worry** no se preocupe [*no say pray-okoopay*]

worse: it's worse es peor [*pay-or*]; **it's getting worse** está cada vez peor [*beth*]

worst el peor [*pay-or*]

worth: it's not worth 500 no vale quinientas [*balay*]; **it's worth more than that** vale más que eso; **is it worth a visit?** ¿vale la pena una visita? [*beeseeta*]

would: would you give this to …? ¿le puede entregar esto a …? [*lay pway-day*]; **what would you do?** ¿qué haría usted? [*kay aree-a oostay*]

wrap: could you wrap it up? ¿me lo envuelve? [*may lo embwelbay*]

wrapping la envoltura [*emb—*]

wrapping paper papel de envolver [*embolbair*]

wrench (*tool*) una llave inglesa [*yabay eenglaysa*]

wrist la muñeca [*moon-yay-ka*]

write escribir; **could you write it down for me?** ¿puede escribírmelo? [*pway-day*]; **how do you write it?** ¿cómo se escribe? [*komo say eskreebay*]; **I'll write to you** le escribiré [*lay eskreebeeray*]; **I wrote to you last month** le escribí el mes pasado

write-off (*car*): **it's a write-off** es una pérdida total [*pairdeeda*]

writer un escritor

writing paper papel de escribir

wrong: you're wrong se equivoca [*say ekeeboka*]; **the bill's wrong** la cuenta está confundida [*kwenta*]; **sorry, wrong number** perdone, me he equivocado de número [*pairdonay, may ay ekeebokado day noomairo*]; **I'm on the wrong train** me he equivocado de tren [*may ay ekeebokado*]; **I went to the wrong room** me equivoqué de habitación [*may ekeebokay*]; **that's the wrong key** no es ésa la llave [*yabay*]; **there's something wrong with …** le pasa algo a …; **what's wrong?** ¿qué pasa?; **what's wrong with it?** ¿qué le pasa?

X-ray una radiografía [*rad-yografee-a*]

---

yacht un yate [*yatay*]

yacht club un club marítimo [*kloob*]

yard: in the yard (*garden*) en el jardín [*Hardeen*] *see page 117*

year un año [*an-yo*]

yellow amarillo [*amaree-yo*]

yellow pages las páginas amarillas [*paHeenas amaree-yas*]

yes sí

yesterday ayer [*a-yair*]; **yesterday morning** ayer por la mañana; **yesterday afternoon** ayer por la tarde; **the day before yesterday** antes de ayer

yet: has it arrived yet? ¿ha llegado ya? [*yegado*]; **not yet** tovavía no [*todabee-a*]

yobo un gamberro

yog(h)urt el yogur

you tú; (*polite form*) usted [*oostay*]; **are you from here?** ¿eres/es de aquí?; **this is for you** esto es para tí/usted [*tee*] *see pages 105, 106*

young joven [*Hoben*]

young people los jóvenes [*Hobenays*]

your tu; (*polite form*) su; **is this your camera?** ¿es tu/su máquina? [*makeena*] *see page 103*

yours tuyo; (*polite form*) suyo; **are these yours?** ¿son tuyos/suyos? *see page 107*

youth hostel un albergue de juventud [*albairgay day Hoobentoo*]

youth hostelling: we're youth hostelling vamos a ir a albergues de juventud [*bamos … albairgays day Hoobentoo*]

Yugoslavia Yugoslavia [*yoogoslab-ya*]

---

zero cero [*thairo*]; **it's below zero** está bajo cero [*baHo*]

zip, zipper una cremallera [*kray-mayai-ra*]; **could you put a new zip on?** ¿po-dría cambiar la cremallera? [*podree-a*]

zoo el jardín zoológico [*Hardeen tho-loHeeko*]

zoom lens el zoom [*soom*]

Spanish–English

A

abierto open

abierto de ... a ... open from ... to ...

abonos season tickets

ábrase aquí open here

ábrase en caso de emergencia open in case of emergency

abrir open

abróchense los cinturones please fasten your seatbelts

academia academy

acantilado cliff

acceso a ... access to ...

acceso a los andenes to the trains

accidente accident

aceite oil

aceitunas *[athay-toonas]* olives

acelgas *[ath-elgas]* saltwort (*similar to lettuce*)

achicoria *[acheekor-ya]* chicory

adelante *[ad-elantay]* come in

adiós *[ad-yos]* goodbye

admisión admission

aduana customs

aerobús local train

aerodeslizador hovercraft

aerolínea airline

aeropuerto airport

agárrese hold on here

agencia de viajes travel agency

agítese antes de usar shake well before using

agua potable drinking water

aguacate *[agwakatay]* avocado

ahumados *[a-oomados]* smoked fish

aire acondicionado air conditioning

alarma alarm

albergue hostel

albóndigas meat balls

alcachofas con jamón *[Hamon]* artichokes with ham

alcachofas salteadas *[saltay-adas]* sauté artichokes

alcachofas vinagreta *[beenagrayta]* artichokes vinaigrette

Alella vine growing area near Barcelona producing red, white and rosé wines

alfombras carpets

algodón cotton

Alicante vine growing area in the south producing red and rosé wines matured in oak casks

alimentación foodstuffs

almacén department store

Almansa vine growing region in the south producing red and white wines

almejas *[almay-Has]* clams

almejas a la marinera *[almay-Has a la mareenaira]* clams stewed in wine and parsley

almejas naturales *[almay-Has natoo-ralays]* live clams

almuerzo lunch

alquiler de coches car rental

alquileres rentals

alto stop

altura máxima maximum headroom

alubias con ... *[aloob-yas]* beans with ...

ambulancia ambulance

ambulatorio national health clinic

a mitad de precio half price

Ampurdàn vine growing region at the foot of the Pyrenees producing only rosé wines

analgésico pain killer

ancas de rana frogs' legs

anchoas *[ancho-as]* anchovies

andén platform, track

anfiteatro amphitheatre

anguila *[angeela]* eel

angulas *[angoolas]* baby eels

anís *[anees]* anis

año ... ... vintage

antes de entrar dejen salir let passengers off first

anticongelante antifreeze

anticuario antiques

anulado cancelled

apague el motor switch off your engine

apague las luces switch off your lights

aparatos electrodomésticos electrical appliances

aparcamiento car park, parking lot

aparcamiento privado private parking

aparcamiento reservado this parking place reserved

aparcamiento vigilado supervised car park, parking lot

apellido surname, family name

arcén lay-by

área de ... ... area

área de servicios service area

arenque [ar-enkay] herring

armería gunsmiths

arroz a la cubana [arroth a la koobana] rice with fried eggs and banana fritters

arroz a la turca [arroth a la toorka] boiled rice with curry sauce, onions and tomatoes

arroz a la valenciana [arroth a la balenth-yana] rice with seafood

arroz con leche [arroth kon lechay] rice pudding

artículos de artesanía arts and crafts

artículos de baño swimwear

artículos de boda wedding presents

artículos de camping camping goods

artículos de deporte sports goods

artículos de limpieza household cleaning products

artículos de ocasión bargains

artículos de piel leather goods

artículos de playa beachwear

artículos de regalo gifts

artículos de viaje travel goods

artículos para el bebé babywear

artículos para el colegio schoolwear

asados roasts

ascensor lift, elevator

aseos toilets, rest rooms

asiento seat

aspirina aspirin

atención please note, take care

atención al tren beware of trains

atún [atoon] tuna

autobús bus

autobús solamente buses only

autocar(es) coach(es), bus(es)

autopista motorway, highway

autopista de peaje toll motorway/ highway

autorizada para mayores de 14 años y menores acompañados authorized for those over fourteen and younger children accompanied by an adult (*film*)

autorizada para mayores (para mayores de ... años) authorized for those over 18 (over ... years of age) (*film*)

autorizada para todos los públicos suitable for all (*film*)

autoservicio self-service

avenida avenue

aviso information

aviso a los señores pasajeros information for passengers

ayuntamiento town hall

azafata air hostess

B

bacalao a la vizcaína [bakala-o a la beethka-eena] cod served with ham, peppers and chilis

bacalao al pil pil [bakala-o al peel peel] cod served with chilis and garlic

bahía bay

banco bank

barbacoa barbecue

barcas para alquilar boats to rent

basura litter

baterías de cocina pots and pans

batido de chocolate [bateedo day chocolatay] chocolate milkshake

batido de fresas [bateedo day fraysas] strawberry milkshake

batido de frutas [bateedo day frootas]

fruit milkshake
batido de vainilla *[bateedo day by-neeya]* vanilla milkshake
bebidas drinks
berenjenas *[bairen-нenas]* aubergines, eggplants
besugo al horno *[besoogo al orno]* baked sea bream
biblioteca library
bicicletas bicycles
bienvenido welcome
billete(s) ticket(s)
bistec de ternera *[beestek day tairnaira]* veal steak
bizcochos *[beethkochos]* sponge fingers
bocadillos *[—dee-yos]* sandwiches
bodegas wine cellars
boite night club
bolsos bags
bomba helada *[bom-ba elada]* sponge with ice cream and meringue

bomberos fire brigade
bonito al horno *[boneeto al orno]* baked tuna fish
bonito con tomate *[boneeto kon tomatay]* tuna with tomato
bonobús book of reduced-price bus tickets
boquerones fritos *[bokay-ronays freetos]* fried anchovies
botiquín first aid box
brazo de gitano *[bratho day нeetano]* Swiss roll
bricolage do-it-yourself
broqueta de riñones *[brokayta day reen-yonays]* kidney kebabs
bufandas scarves
buñuelos *[boon-ywaylos]* light fried pastry
butacas stalls
butifarra *[booteefarra]* Catalan sausage
buzón letter box

C

c/ (calle) street
caballeros gents, men's rest room
cabida ... personas capacity ... people
cabina telefónica telephone booth
cabrito asado roast kid
¡cabrón! bastard!
cachelada *[kachay-lada]* pork stew with eggs, tomato and onion
caduca ... expires on ...
café coffee
café con leche white coffee, coffee with milk
cafeteras coffee pots
cafetería cafe
caja cash point
caja de ahorros savings bank
cajero cashier
calamares a la romana *[kalamarays]* squid rings in batter
calamares en su tinta *[kalamarays en soo teenta]* squid cooked in their ink
calamares fritos *[kalamarays freetos]*

fried squid
calculadoras calculators
caldeirada *[kalday-rada]* fish soup
caldereta gallega *[kalday-rayta gayayga]* vegetable stew
caldo de ... ... soup
caldo gallina *[ga-yeena]* chicken soup
caldo gallego *[ga-yaygo]* vegetable soup
caldo guanche *[gwanchay]* soup made with potatoes, onions, tomatoes and courgettes/zucchinis
caliente hot
calle street
callejón sin salida cul de sac, dead-end
callos a la madrileña *[ka-yos a la madreelayn-ya]* tripe cooked with chilis
calzada deteriorada poor road surface
camarera chambermaid, maid; waitress
camareros waiters
camarones *[kamaronays]* baby prawns
camarote(s) cabin(s)

cambio (rate of) exchange
cambio de sentido take filter lane to cross flow of traffic
camino cerrado road closed
camisería shirts
camisetas T-shirts, vests
camping camp site
Campsa state owned oil company
caña (cerveza) 250cc (of beer)
Canal de la Mancha English Channel
Canarias Canary Islands
canelones [kanay-lonays] cannelloni
cangrejos de río [kang-gray-нos day ree-o] river crabs
cantina buffet
capilla protestante Protestant chapel
caracoles [karakolays] snails
caramelos sweets, candies
carbonada de buey [day bway] beef cooked in beer
Cariñena vine growing region in the north producing red and rosé wines
carnes [karnays] meats
carnicería butcher
carpintería joiner, carpenter
carretera comarcal district highway
carretera cortada road blocked
carretera de circunvalación by-pass
carretera de doble calzada dual carriageway, divided highway
carretera nacional national highway
carretera principal main highway
carro de queso [kayso] cheese board
carta menu
cartas letters
cartelera de espectáculos entertainments guide
casa de socorro first aid centre
castañas [kastan-yas] chestnuts
castillo castle
Cataluña Catalonia
catedral cathedral
c/c (cuenta corriente) current account
ceda el paso give way, yield
cementerio cemetery
cena dinner
centollo [thento-yo] spider crab
centro ciudad city centre/center
cerámica ceramics
cerrado closed
cerrado por defunción closed due to bereavement
cerrado por descanso del personal

closed for staff holidays
cerrado por obras closed for alterations
cerrado por reforma closed for renovation
cerrado por vacaciones closed: on holiday/vacation
cervecería bar
cerveza [thairbaytha] beer
CH (casa de huéspedes) low-price hostel, rooming house
chalecos salvavidas life-jackets
champaña [champan-ya] champagne
champiñón [champeen-yon] mushroom
chanfaina [chanfa-eena] rice and black pudding/blood sausage stew
chanquetes [chankaytays] fish (similar to whitehead)
chaquetas jackets
charcutería delicatessen
chateaubrian chateaubriand steak
cheques de viaje travellers' cheques, travelers' checks
Cheste vine growing area to the west of Valencia producing dry and sweet white wines
chipirones [cheepeeronays] squid
chipirones en su tinta [cheepeeronays en soo teenta] squid cooked in their own ink
chipirones rellenos [cheepeeronays ray-yaynos] stuffed squid
chuleta de buey [choolayta day bway] beef chop
chuleta de cerdo [choolayta day thairdo] pork chop
chuleta de cerdo empanada [choolayta day thairdo] breaded pork chop
chuleta de cordero [choolayta day kordairo] lamb chop
chuleta de ternera [choolayta day tairnaira] veal chop
chuleta de ternera empanada [choolayta day tairnaira] breaded veal chop
chuletas de lomo ahumado [choolaytas day lomo a-oomado] smoked pork chops
chuletitas de cordero [choolay-teetas day kordairo] small lamb chops
chuletón [choolayton] large chop
chuletón de buey [choolayton day bway] large beef chop
churros [choorros] fried pastry cut into lengths
Cía. (compañía) company

cierren las puertas please close the doors
cigalas *[theegalas]* cray fish
cinturones belts
circulación en ambas direcciones two way traffic
circule por la derecha keep to your right
ciudad city, town
coca amb pinxes *[koka am peenshis]* sardine pie (*Catalonia*)
coche-cama sleeping car
coche-comedor dining car
coche-restaurante restaurant car
coches de niño prams, baby-strollers
cochinillo asado *[kocheenee-yo]* roast suckling pig
cocido castellano *[kotheedo kastay-yano]* stew made with meat, chickpeas, vegetables etc
cóctel de bogavante *[bogabantay]* lobster cocktail
cocochas (de merluza) *[mairlootha]* hake stew
cóctel de gambas prawn cocktail
cóctel de langostinos *[lang-gosteenos]* king prawn cocktail
cóctel de mariscos seafood cocktail
codornices *[kodorneethays]* quail
colchas bedspreads
colegio school
coles de bruselas *[kolays day broosay-las]* brussels sprouts
coliflor cauliflower
combustible fuel
comedor dining room
comidas para llevar take-away
comisaría de policía police station
completo full
comprimido efervescente soluble tablet
comprimidos pills
con receta médica only available on prescription
coñács cognacs
Conca de Barbera vine growing region in Catalonia producing red and white wines
Condado de Huelva vine growing region in the south producing dry, mellow and sweet white wines
conduzca con cuidado drive with care
conejo asado *[konay-ho]* roast rabbit
conejo encebollado *[konay-ho enthebo-yado]* rabbit served with onions
confección de caballero menswear

confección de señoras ladies' fashions
confecciones ready to wear clothes
conferencia interurbana trunk call, long distance call
conferencias internacionales international calls
confitería sweets, candies
congelados frozen foods
congrio conger eel
¡coño! damn!
conserje janitor, porter
conservas *[konsairbas]* jams, preserves
consigna left luggage, baggage checkroom
consomé al jeréz *[konsomay al Haireth]* consommé with sherry
consomé con yema *[konsomay]* consommé with egg yolk
consomé de ave *[konsomay day abay]* chicken consommé
consomé de pollo *[konsomay day po-yo]* chicken consommé
consulado consulate
consulta médica surgery, doctor's office
consúmase antes de ... best before ...
contenido contents
contra de ternera con guisantes *[tairnaira kon g-eesantays]* veal stew with peas
contrafilete de ternera *[tairnaira]* veal fillet
contraindicaciones contra-indications
convento convent
copa glass
corbatas ties, neckties
cordero asado *[kordairo]* roast lamb
cordero chilindrón *[kordairo cheeleendron]* lamb stew with onion, tomato, peppers and eggs
correo mail
correo aéreo air mail
Correos y Telégrafos Post Office
corrida de toros bull fight
corrimiento de tierras danger: landslides
corsetería corsets
cosecha vintage
cosméticos cosmetics
costillas de cerdo *[kostee-yas day thairdo]* pork ribs
crédito credit
crema catalana crème brûlée, crème caramel

crema de cangrejos *[kang-gray-Hos]* cream of crab soup

crema de espárragos cream of asparagus soup

crema de legumbres/verduras *[leg-oombrays, bairdooras]* cream of vegetable soup

cremada dessert made with egg, sugar and milk

cremalleras zips, zippers

crêpe imperial *[eempair-yal]* crepe suzette

criadillas de tierra *[kree-adee-yas day t-yairra]* ground tubers

cristalería glassware

crocante ice cream with chopped nuts

croquetas *[krokaytas]* croquettes

cruce junction, intersection

cruce de ciclistas danger: cyclists crossing

cruce de ganado danger: cattle crossing

Cruz Roja Red Cross

cuajada *[kwa-Hada]* curds

cuartel de la guardia civil civil guard barracks

cuarto piso (*UK*) fourth floor, (*USA*) fifth floor

cuchillería cutlery, flatware

cuentas corrientes current accounts

cuidado *[kweedado]* take care

cuidado con el escalón please mind the step

cuidado con el perro beware of the dog

cuneta hard shoulder

curva bend

curva peligrosa dangerous bend

D

d. (don) Mr.

damas ladies' toilet, ladies' rest room

dcha. (derecha) right

décimo piso (*UK*) tenth floor, (*USA*) eleventh floor

decoración interior decoration

... de etiqueta formal ...

de lujo luxury

de nada you're welcome

dentista dentist

departamento de ... ... department

desayuno breakfast

descuelgue el auricular lift the receiver

descuentos discounts

descuentos especiales special discounts

desinfectante disinfectant

despacho de billetes ticket office

desprendimiento de terreno danger: landslides

destino destination

desviación diversion

desvío detour

de venta aquí on sale here

diario daily

dibujos animados cartoons

dígame *[deegamay]* hello, yes

dirección única one way traffic

disco obligatorio parking disk must be displayed

discos records

discoteca discotheque

disculpen las molestias we apologize for any inconvenience

disuélvase en agua dissolve in water

dólar dollar

donaciones donations

droguería drugstore

duchas showers

E

EE.UU. (Estados Unidos) USA
ebanistería cabinetmaker
edredones eiderdowns, duvets
el uso del tabaco es perjudicial para su salud smoking can damage your health
electricista electrician
electrodomésticos electrical appliances
embajada embassy
embarque embarcation
embotellado en ... bottled in ...
embutidos *[embooteedos]* sausages
emergencias casualty, emergencies
empanada gallega *[ga-yayga]* fish pie
empanada santiaguesa *[sant-yagwaysa]* fish pie
empanadillas de bonito *[empanadee-yas]* small tuna pies
empanadillas de carne *[empanadee-yas day karnay]* meat pies
empanadillas de chorizo *[empanadee-yas day choreetho]* spiced sausage pies
empaquetado packing
empleado employee
empujar push
encienda las luces switch on your lights
enlatados canned goods
ensalada de arenque *[a-renkay]* fish salad
ensalada de atún *[atoon]* tuna salad
ensalada de frutas *[frootas]* fruit salad
ensalada de gambas prawn salad
ensalada de lechuga *[lechooga]* lettuce salad
ensalada de pollo *[po-yo]* chicken salad
ensalada de tomate *[tomatay]* tomato salad
ensalada ilustrada *[eeloostrada]* mixed salad
ensalada mixta *[meesta]* mixed salad
ensalada simple *[seemplay]* green salad
ensaladilla *[ensaladee-ya]* Spanish salad
ensaladilla rusa *[ensaladee-ya roosa]* Russian salad
entrada way in
entrada libre admission/entry free
entradas tickets
entradas starters
entre sin llamar enter without knocking
entreacto intermission
entrecot a la parrilla *[entraykot a la parree-ya]* grilled entrecote
entrecot de ternera *[entraykot day tairnaira]* veal entrecote
entremeses de la casa *[entray-maysays]* hors d'oeuvres
entremeses variados *[entray-maysays bar-yados]* hors d'oeuvres
equipajes baggage
es peligroso asomarse al exterior do not lean out
es peligroso bañarse danger: no swimming
escalera automática escalator
escalón lateral ramp, uneven road surface
escalope a la milanesa *[eskalopay]* breaded veal with cheese
escalope a la parrilla *[eskalopay a la parree-ya]* grilled veal
escalope a la plancha *[eskalopay]* grilled veal
escalope de lomo de cerdo *[eskalopay ... thairdo]* escalope of fillet of pork
escalope de ternera *[eskalopay day tairnaira]* escalope of veal
escalope empanado *[eskalopay]* breaded escalope
escalopines al vino de Marsala *[eskalopeenays al beeno]* veal escalopes cooked in wine
escalopines de ternera *[eskalopeenays day tairnaira]* veal escalopes
escarola curly lettuce
Escocia Scotland
escuela school

escuela de párvulos kindergarten

escurrir a mano wring by hand

espadín a la toledana *[espadeen a la tolay-dana]* kebab

espaguetis italiana *[espagetees eetal-yana]* spaghetti

España Spain

espárragos asparagus

espárragos con mayonesa/mahonesa *[ma-onaysa]* asparagus with mayonnaise

especialidades special(i)ties

especialista en ... specialist in ...

espectáculo de luz y sonido spectacle of light and sound, son et lumière

espejos mirrors

esperar, espere please wait

espinacas a la crema spinach a la crème

espinazo de cerdo con patatas *[espee-natho day thairdo]* pork ribs with potatoes *(stew)*

espumoso *[espoomoso]* sparkling *(wine)*

esta tienda se traslada a ... business is being transferred to ...

estación de autobuses bus station

estación de servicio service station

estación de trenes train station

estacionamiento limitado restricted parking

estacionamiento vigilado supervised parking

estadio de fútbol football stadium

Estados Unidos United States

estanco tobacconist, tobacco store *(also sells stamps)*

esterilizada sterilized

estofado de ... ... stew

estofado de liebre *[l-yaybray]* hare stew

estofados stews

estrechamiento de calzada road narrows

estreno new film release

ETA Basque terrorist organization

excepto ... except ...

excepto domingos y festivos except Sundays and holidays

excepto sábados except Saturdays

exceso de equipaje excess baggage

excursión a ... trip to ...

excursiones con guía guided tours

exportación export

exposición exhibition

extranjero overseas, abroad

F

fabada (asturiana) bean stew with sausage

fabricado por ... made by ...

factura bill

facturación check-in

faisán con castañas *[fa-eesan kon kastan-yas]* pheasant with chestnuts

faisán estofado *[fa-eesan]* stewed pheasant

faisán trufado *[fa-eesan troofado]* pheasant with truffles

fajas corsets

farmacia chemist, pharmacy

farmacia de guardia emergency chemist/pharmacy

fecha de caduación expiry date

fecha de caducidad expiry date

fecha límite de venta sell-by date

feria de ... ... fair

ferretería ironmonger, hardware store

fiambres cold meats, cold cuts

fibras naturales natural fibres/fibers

fideos *[feeday-os]* thin pasta, noodles

fiesta de ... feast of ... (saint)

fila row

filete a la parrilla *[feelay-tay a la parree-ya]* grilled beef steak

filete de cerdo *[feelay-tay day thairdo]* pork steak

filete de ternera *[feelay-tay day tair-naira]* veal steak

fin de ... end of ...

fin de serie discontinued articles
final de autopista end of motorway/highway
firme deslizante slippery road surface
flan crème caramel
flan al ron crème caramel with rum
flan de caramelo crème caramel
flores flowers
floristería florist
flotadores lifebelts
fontanería plumber
fotografía photography

fotógrafo photographer
fresas con nata strawberries with cream
frigoríficos fridges
frío cold
fruta fruit
fruta variada *[bar-yada]* fruit
frutas en almíbar *[frootas en almeebar]* fruit in syrup
frutería fruit shop/store
fuera de servicio out of order
fumadores smokers
funeraria undertaker, mortician

G

gabardinas raincoats
gafas spectacles
galería gallery
galería de arte art gallery
galerías store
Gales Wales
galletas biscuits, cookies
gallina a la cairatraca *[ga-yeena a la ka-eeratraka]* stewed chicken
gallina en pepitoria *[ga-yeena em pepeetor-ya]* stewed chicken with peppers
gambas a la americana prawns
gambas a la plancha grilled prawns
gambas al ajillo *[a-Hee-yo]* prawns with garlic
gambas cocidas *[kotheedas]* boiled prawns
gambas con mayonesa prawns with mayonnaise
gambas en gabardina prawns in batter
gambas rebozadas *[rebothadas]* prawns in batter
gangas bargains
garaje garage
garantía guarantee
garbanzos *[garbanthos]* chickpeas
garbanzos a la catalana *[garbanthos]* chickpeas with sausage, boiled eggs and pine kernels
gas-oil diesel
gasolina normal two-star petrol, regular

(gas)
gasolina super four-star petrol, premium
(gas)
gasolinera petrol/gas station
gazpacho andaluz *[gathpacho andalooth]* cold vegetable soup
gazpacho manchego *[gathpacho manchaygo]* rabbit stew with tomato and garlic (sometimes also with partridge meat)
gelatina de ... *[Helateena day]* ... jelly
¡gilipollas! *[Heeleepo-yas]* stupid bastard!
ginebra *[Heenaybra]* gin
giros money orders
gorros de baño swimming caps
gorros de niño children's bonnets
gotas drops
gótico Gothic
gracias *[grath-yas]* thank you
Gran Bretaña Great Britain
grandes almacenes large department stores
grandes rebajas prices slashed
gratén de ... *[grat-en day]* ... au gratin, with a thick cheese sauce
gratis free
gravilla loose chippings
guantes gloves
guardacostas coastguard
guardarropa cloakroom, checkroom
guardería crèche

guerra civil civil war
guía guide
guía telefónica telephone directory

guía turística tourist guide
guisantes con jamón [g-eesantays kon ᴴamon] peas with ham

H

habas [abas] beans
habichuelas [abeechway-las] kidney beans
habitación doble double room
habitación individual single room
hable aquí speak here
hágalo Usted mismo do-it-yourself
hay ... we sell ...
heladería ice creams
helado de caramelo [elado] caramel ice cream
helado de chocolate [elado day chocolatay] chocolate ice cream
helado de fresa [elado] strawberry ice cream
helado de mantecado [elado] vanilla ice cream
helado de nata [elado] vanilla ice cream
helado de vainilla [elado day ba-eeneeya] vanilla ice cream
herramientas tools
hígado [eegado] liver
higos con miel y nueces [eegos kon m-yel ee nwaythays] figs with honey and nuts
hipermercado hypermarket
hipódromo hippodrome
hogar household goods
hombres men
horario de autobuses bus timetable/schedule
horario de invierno winter timetable/schedule
horario de trenes train timetable/schedule
horario de verano summer timetable/schedule
horas de consulta surgery hours, office hours (of doctor)
horas de visita visiting hours

horchata (de chufas) [orchata day choofas] almond-flavo(u)red milk drink
hornazo [ornazo] Easter pie
hostal boarding house
HR (hostal-residencia) boarding house where no meals are served, often lower-priced
huevo hilado [waybo eelado] shredded boiled eggs used as a garnish
huevos [waybos] eggs
huevos a la flamenca [waybos] fried eggs with ham, tomato and vegetables
huevos cocidos [waybos kotheedos] hard boiled eggs
huevos con jamón [waybos kon ᴴamon] eggs with ham
huevos con mayonesa [waybos] boiled eggs with mayonnaise
huevos con panceta [waybos kon panthayta] eggs with bacon
huevos con patatas fritas [waybos] fried eggs and chips/French fries
huevos con picadillo [waybos kon peekadee-yo] eggs with sausage meat
huevos con salchichas [waybos kon salcheechas] eggs and sausages
huevos escalfados [waybos] poached eggs
huevos fritos [waybos] fried eggs
huevos fritos con chorizo [waybos ... choreetho] fried eggs with Spanish sausage
huevos fritos con jamón [waybos ... kon ᴴamon] fried eggs with ham
huevos pasados por agua [waybos ... agwa] boiled eggs
huevos rellenos [waybos re-yaynos] stuffed eggs
huevos revueltos con tomate [waybos rebweltos kon tomatay] scrambled eggs with tomato

I

iglesia church
impermeables waterproofs
importación imported goods
importe amount
importe total total due
incluye pan, postre y vino *[eenkloo-yay pan postray ee beeno]* includes bread, dessert and wine
indicaciones instructions for use ...
infantil children's ...
inflamable inflammable
información information
información de vuelos flight information
información y turismo tourist information
infusiones herb teas
Inglaterra England
ingredientes ingredients
ingresos deposits
inserte moneda insert coin
instituto de belleza beauty salon
instrucciones de lavado washing instructions
intermedio intermission
introduzca moneda insert coin
Irlanda Ireland
IVA (impuesto sobre el valor añadido) VAT
izq. (izquierda) left

J

jabones soaps
jamón serrano *[намon sairrano]* cured ham
jamonería hams
jarabe syrup
jardinería gardening
jarra de vino *[нarra day beeno]* wine jug
jerez amontillado *[нaireth amontee-yado]* pale dry sherry
jerez fino *[нaireth feeno]* pale light sherry
jerez oloroso *[нaireth]* sweet sherry
jeta *[нeta]* pigs' cheeks
¡joder! *[нodair]* hell!
joyería jewe(l)lery
judías verdes *[нoodee-as bairdays]* French beans
judías verdes a la española *[нoodee-as bairdays a la espan-yola]* French bean stew
judías verdes con jamón *[нoodee-as bairdays kon намon]* French beans with ham
jugo de albaricoque *[нoogo day albareekokay]* apricot juice
jugo de lima *[нoogo]* lime juice
jugo de limón *[нoogo]* lemon juice
jugo de melocotón *[нoogo]* peach juice
jugo de naranja *[нoogo day naran-нa]* orange juice
jugo de piña *[нoogo day peen-ya]* pineapple juice
jugo de tomate *[нoogo day tomatay]* tomato juice
juguetería toy shop/store
juguetes toys
Jumilla vine growing region in the south producing red, dry light red and sweet white wines

K

kilómetro kilometre/kilometer
km/h (kilómetros/hora) kilometres/

kilometers per hour
kv (kilovatios) kilowatts

L

la vuelta al colegio back to school
lacón con grelos shoulder of pork with turnip tops
lámparas lamps
lana pura pure wool
lanas wools
lanas al peso wool sold by weight
langosta a la americana lobster with brandy and garlic
langosta a la catalana lobster with mushrooms and ham in a bechamel sauce (*white sauce made from cream, butter and flour*)
langosta fría con mayonesa cold lobster with mayonnaise
langosta gratinada lobster au gratin (*in a thick cheese sauce*)
langostinos a la plancha grilled king prawns
langostinos con mayonesa king prawns with mayonnaise
langostinos dos salsas king prawns cooked in two sauces
latas canned goods
lavabos toilets, rest rooms
lavandería laundry
lavaplatos dishwashers
lavar a mano wash by hand
lavar en seco dry clean
lavar separadamente wash separately
leche frita [*lechay freeta*] pudding with milk and eggs

leche merengada [*lechay*] cold milk with meringues
lechería dairy produce
lencería drapery
lengua de buey [*leng-gwa day bway*] ox tongue
lengua de cordero estofada [*leng-gwa day kordairo*] stewed lamb tongue
lenguado a la parrilla [*leng-gwado a la parree-ya*] grilled sole
lenguado a la plancha [*leng-gwado*] grilled sole
lenguado a la romana [*leng-gwado*] sole in batter
lenguado frito [*leng-gwado*] fried sole
lenguado grillado [*leng-gwado gree-yado*] grilled sole
lenguado meuniere [*leng-gwado*] sole meunière
lentejas aliñadas [*lentay-Has aleen-yadas*] lentils with vinaigrette
lentejas onubenses [*lentay-Has onoobensays*] lentils with spiced sausage, onion and garlic
leotardos tights
letra draft
libra pound
libre free
librería bookshop, bookstore
libreta de ahorros savings account book
libros books

libros de bolsillo paperbacks
licor de manzana *[leekor day manthana]* apple liqueur
licor de pera *[leekor day paira]* pear liqueur
licores *[leekorays]* spirits, liquors; liqueurs
liebre estofada *[l-yebray]* stewed hare
límite de altura height limit
límite de peso weight limit
límite de velocidad speed limit
limpieza de coches car wash
limpieza en seco dry-cleaning
liquidación total clearance sale
lista de correos poste restante, general delivery
lista de espera standby
lista de precios price list
listas de boda wedding lists
literas couchettes
litros litres
llamada call
llame a la puerta please knock
llame al timbre please ring

llaves keys
llegadas arrivals
llegadas internacionales international arrivals
llegadas nacionales domestic arrivals
lleno, por favor *[yay-no]* fill her up, please
localidades tickets
lombarda rellena *[ray-yayna]* stuffed red cabbage
lombarda salteada *[saltay-ada]* sauté red cabbage
lomo curado *[koorado]* cured pork sausage
lonchas de jamón *[Hamon]* cured ham (sliced)
Londres London
loza crockery
lubina a la marinera *[loobeena a la mareenaira]* sea bass in a parsley sauce
lubina al horno *[loobeena al orno]* baked sea bass
lunes Monday
luz de cruce dipped headlights, low beam

M

macarrones macaroni
macarrones gratinados macaroni cheese
Málaga vine growing region on the south coast producing sweet and dry white wines
maletas suitcases
Mancha vine growing region of the interior (the largest vine growing region in Spain) producing mainly white, but also red and pale red wines
manises *[maneesays]* peanuts
manitas de cordero *[kordairo]* shank of lamb
manos de cerdo *[thairdo]* pigs' trotters
manos de cerdo a la parrilla *[thairdo a la parree-ya]* grilled pigs' trotters
mantas blankets
mantecadas small sponge cakes

mantelerías table linen
mantenga limpia España keep Spain tidy
mantenga limpia la ciudad keep our city tidy
manténgase alejado de los niños keep out of the reach of children
manténgase en sitio fresco store in a cool place
mantequilla *[mantay-kee-ya]* butter
manzanas *[manthanas]* apples
manzanas asadas *[manthanas]* baked apples
manzanilla *[manthanee-ya]* dry sherry-type wine, camomile tea
mapas maps
maquillaje make-up
máquina tragaperras slot machine
maquinaria machinery

maquinaria pesada heavy machinery
máquinas de ... ... machines
marca registrada registered trade mark
marcar el número dial the number
mariscada cold mixed shellfish
mariscos del día fresh shellfish
mariscos del tiempo seasonal shellfish
marisquería shellfish restaurant
marroquinería fancy leather goods
máximo personas maximum number of people
mazapán [mathapan] marzipan
¡me cago en diez! [d-yayth] for Christ's sake!
mecánico mechanic
medallones de anguila [meda-yonays day angeela] eel steaks
medallones de merluza [meda-yonays day mairlootha] hake steaks
media de agua [maid-ya day agwa] half-bottle of mineral water
media pensión half board, European plan
médico doctor
mejillones [me-нee-yonays] mussels
mejillones a la marinera [mee-нee-yonays a la mareenaira] mussels in a wine sauce
melocotón peach
melocotones en almíbar peaches in syrup
melón con jamón [нamon] melon with ham
membrillo [membree-yo] quince jelly
menestra de legumbres [legoombrays] vegetable stew
Mentrida vine growing region of the interior producing deep coloured red wines
menú de la casa [menoo] fixed price menu
menú del día [menoo] set menu
mercado market
mercería haberdashery, notions
merluza a la cazuela [mairlootha a la kathway-la] stewed hake
merluza a la parrilla [mairlootha a la parree-ya] grilled hake
merluza a la plancha [mairlootha] grilled hake
merluza a la riojana [mairlootha a la r-yoнana] hake with chilis
merluza a la romana [mairlootha] hake steaks in batter

merluza a la vasca [mairlootha a la baska] hake in a garlic sauce
merluza al ajo arriero [mairlootha al aнo arr-yairo] hake with garlic and chilis
merluza en salsa [mairlootha] hake in sauce
merluza en salsa verde [mairlootha en salsa bairday] hake in a parsley and wine sauce
merluza fría [mairlootha free-a] cold hake
merluza frita [mairlootha] fried hake
mermelada [mairmelada] jam
mermelada de albaricoque [mairmelada day albareekokay] apricot jam
mermelada de ciruelas [mairmelada day theerwaylas] plum jam
mermelada de frambuesas [mairmelada day frambway-sas] raspberry jam
mermelada de fresas [mairmelada] strawberry jam
mermelada de limón [mairmelada] lemon marmalade
mermelada de melocotón [mairmelada] peach jam
mermelada de naranja [mairmelada day naran-нa] orange marmalade
mero [mairo] grouper (fish)
mero a la parrilla [mairo a la parree-ya] grilled grouper
mero en salsa verde [mairo en salsa bairday] grouper with garlic and parsley sauce
mesón inn
metro underground
mezquita mosque
microbús minibus
¡mierda! [m-yairda] shit!
ministerio de ... ministry of ...
mirador scenic view, vantage point
mitad de precio half price
moda jóvenes young fashions
moda juvenil young fashions
modas caballeros gents' fashions
modas niños/niñas children's fashions
modas pre-mamá maternity fashions
modas señora ladies' fashions
modista dressmaker
modo de empleo instructions for use
mollejas de ternera fritas [mo-yay-нas day tairnaira] fried sweetbreads
montacargas service lift

Montilla-Moriles vine growing region in Andalusia producing sherry-like white wines

moquetas carpets

morcilla *[morthee-ya]* black pudding, blood sausage

morcilla de carnero *[morthee-ya day karnairo]* black pudding/blood sausage made from mutton

moros Moors

morros de cerdo *[thairdo]* pigs' cheeks

morros de vaca *[baka]* cheeks of beef

morteruelo *[mortair-waylo]* kind of mince pie/ground beef pie

mousse de ... ... mousse

muchas gracias *[moochas grath-yas]* thank you very much

muebles furniture

muebles de cocina kitchen furniture

muelle quay

multa fine

museo museum

N

N (carretera nacional) national highway (*always followed by a number*)

nada que declarar nothing to declare

nata cream

natillas *[natee-yas]* cold custard

natillas de chocolate *[natee-yas day chocolatay]* cold custard with chocolate

Navarra vine growing region in the north producing dry white and fruity red and rosé wines

neumáticos — se reparan, se arreglan tyres/tires repaired

niebla fog

niños/niñas children

no admite plancha do not iron

no aparcar no parking

no aparcar, llamamos grúa illegally parked vehicles will be towed away

no contiene alcohol does not contain alcohol

no exceda la dosis indicada do not exceed the stated dose

no fumadores non-smokers

no funciona out of order

no hay localidades sold out

no molestar do not disturb

no pisar el césped keep off the grass

no recomendada para menores de 18 años not recommended for those under 18 years of age (*film*)

no se admiten caravanas/perros no caravans/dogs allowed

no tocar please do not touch

no utilizar lejía do not bleach

ñoquis *[n-yokees]* potato-based pasta

norte north

novelas novels

noveno piso (*UK*) ninth floor, (*USA*) tenth floor

novillada bullfight featuring novice bullfighters

Nueva York New York

O

objetos de ... ... goods
objetos perdidos lost and found, lost property
obras roadwork(s)
octavo piso *(UK)* eighth floor, *(USA)* ninth floor
oculista optician
ocupado engaged, occupied
oferta (especial) special offer
oficina de ... ... office
oficina de correos post office
oficina de objetos perdidos lost property office, lost and found
oficina de reclamaciones complaints department
oficina de registros registrar's office
ojo al tren beware of the train
oportunidades bargains
óptico optician
orejas de cerdo *[oray-ʜas day thairdo]* pigs' ears
otros mariscos según precios en plaza other shellfish depending on current prices

P

p (paseo) street
paella *[pa-eya]* fried rice with various shellfish and chicken
paella castellana *[pa-eya kastay-yana]* fried rice with meat
paella de marisco *[pa-eya]* fried rice with shellfish
paella de pollo *[pa-eya day po-yo]* fried rice with chicken
paella valenciana *[pa-eya balenth-yana]* fried rice with various shellfish and chicken
pagadero payable
pagos deposits
País Vasco Basque Country
palacio de ... ... palace
palacio de congresos conference hall
palacio real royal palace
palco box *(at theatre)*
paleta de cordero lechal *[kordairo]* shoulder of lamb
palomitas de maíz *[ma-eeth]* popcorn
pan bread
panaché de verduras *[panachay day bairdooras]* vegetable stew
panadería bakery
pañales nappies, diapers
panceta *[panthay-ta]* bacon
pañería drapery
pantalones trousers, pants
pantalones vaqueros jeans
pañuelos handkerchiefs
papelería stationery
papeles pintados wallpaper
paquete packet
para automáticas for automatic washing machines
para uso del personal staff only
parada stop
parada de autobuses bus stop
parada de taxis taxi rank
parador nacional state owned hotel,

often a historic building which has been restored

paraguas umbrellas
parking car park, parking lot
parque park
parque de atracciones amusement park
parque de bomberos fire station
parque infantil children's park
parrilla grillroom
parrillada de caza *[parree-yada day katha]* mixed grilled game
parrillada de mariscos *[parree-yada]* mixed grilled shellfish
particular private
pasajeros de tránsito transit passengers
pasaportes passport control
pasen enter; cross, walk
paseo de ... ... avenue
paso a nivel level crossing, grade crossing
paso a nivel no vigilado unmanned level crossing/grade crossing
paso a nivel vigilado manned level crossing/grade crossing
paso de peatones pedestrian crossing
paso subterráneo underpass
pastel de ... ... cake, pie
pastel de ternera *[tairnaira]* veal pie
pastelería cake shop/store
pasteles cakes
pasteurizada pasteurized
pastillas para ... ... pills
patatas a la pescadora potatoes with fish
patatas asadas roast potatoes
patatas bravas *[brabas]* potatoes in cayenne sauce
patatas fritas chips, French fries; crisps, potato chips
patio de butacas stalls
patitos rellenos *[ray-yaynos]* stuffed duckling
pato a la naranja *[naran-ʜa]* duck a l'orange
pato asado roast duck
pato estofado stewed duck
pavipollo *[pabeepo-yo]* large chicken
pavo asado *[pabo]* roast turkey
pavo relleno *[pabo ray-yayno]* stuffed turkey
pavo trufado *[pabo troofado]* turkey stuffed with truffles
peaje toll
peatones caminen por la izquierda pedestrians please keep to the left

pecho de ternera *[tairnaira]* breast of veal
pechuga de pollo *[pechoooga day po-yo]* breast of chicken
peixo-palo a la marinera *[pesho ... mareenaira]* stock-fish with potatoes and tomato
peletería furs
peligro danger
peligro de incendio danger: fire hazard
peluquería (de caballeros, de señoras) (gents', ladies') hairdresser
pendiente de pago outstanding (*bill, payment*)
Penedés vine growing region in Catalonia producing in particular sparkling white wines
pensión boarding house
pensión completa full board, American plan
pepinillos *[pepeenee-yos]* gherkins
pepino cucumber
percebes *[pairthaybes]* shellfish (*edible barnacle*)
perdices a la campesina *[pairdeethays]* partridges with vegetables
perdices a la manchega *[pairdeethays]* partridges in red wine with garlic, herbs and peppers
perdices asadas *[pairdeethays]* roast partridges
perdices con chocolate *[pairdeethays kon chokolatay]* partridges with chocolate
perdices escabechadas *[pairdeethays]* marinated partridges
perdices estofadas *[pairdeethays]* stewed partridges
perdón *[pairdon]* sorry, excuse me
perejil *[pairay-ʜeel]* parsley
perfumería perfumes
pesca fishing
pescadería fishmonger
pescaditos fritos fried fish
peseta peseta, Spanish unit of currency
peso máximo maximum weight
peso neto net weight
pestiños *[pesteen-yos]* sugared pastries with anis
pez espada ahumado *[peth espada a-oomado]* smoked swordfish
picadillo de ternera *[peekadee-yo day tairnaira]* minced veal

pichones estofados *[peechonays]* stewed pigeon

piezas de recambio spares

pijamas pyjamas, pajamas

pimientos fritos *[peem-yentos]* fried peppers

pimientos morrones *[peem-yentos]* strong peppers

pimientos rellenos *[peem-yentos ray-yaynos]* stuffed peppers

piña al gratén *[peen-ya]* pineapple au gratin (*with a thick cheese sauce*)

piña fresca *[peen-ya]* fresh pineapple

pinchos snacks served in bars

pinchos morunos *[moroonos]* kebabs

pintada guinea fowl

pintura paints

piparrada vasca *[basca]* pepper and tomato stew with ham and eggs

Pirineos Pyrenees

piscina swimming pool

piso amueblado furnished flat/apartment

piso sin amueblar unfurnished flat/apartment

pista de baile dance floor

pista de patinaje skating rink

pista de tenis tennis court

pistas de esquí ski runs

pisto manchego marrow with onion and tomato

planta baja (*UK*) ground floor, (*USA*) first floor

planta primera (*UK*) first floor, (*USA*) second floor

plantas plants

plátanos bananas

plátanos flameados bananas flambé

platos combinados mixture of various foods served as one dish

plaza de toros bullring

plazas libres seats available

policía police

policía municipal municipal police

pollo a la parrilla *[po-yo a la parree-ya]* grilled chicken

pollo a la riojana *[po-yo a la r-yoнana]* chicken with peppers and chilis

pollo al ajillo *[po-yo al aнee-yo]* fried chicken with garlic

pollo al vino blanco *[po-yo al beeno]* chicken in white wine

pollo asado *[po-yo]* roast chicken

pollo braseado *[po-yo brasay-ado]* braised chicken

pollo con tomate *[po-yo kon tomatay]* chicken with tomatoes

pollo con verduras *[po-yo kon bairdooras]* chicken and vegetables

pollo en cacerola *[po-yo en kathairola]* chicken casserole

pollo en pepitoria *[po-yo]* chicken in wine with saffron, garlic and almonds

pollo salteado *[po-yo]* chicken sauté

pollos tomateros con zanahorias *[po-yos tomatairos kon thana-oryas]* young chicken with carrots

polvorones *[polboronays]* sugar-based sweet (*eaten at Christmas*)

por favor *[por fabor]* please

porcelana porcelain

por la otra puerta use other door

portero porter

por vía aérea by air mail

posada inn

postales postcards

potaje castellano *[potaнay kastay-yano]* thick broth

precaución take care

precio price

precio total total price

precio unidad unit price

precios fijos fixed prices

prefijo dialling code, area code

prendas clothing

primer piso (*UK*) first floor, (*USA*) second floor

primera clase first class

principio de autopista start of motorway/highway

Priorato vine growing region near Tarragona

prioridad a la derecha give way/yield to vehicles coming from your right

prioridad de paso priority

privado private

producido en ... produce of ...

producto preparado con ingredientes naturales product prepared using natural ingredients

productos alimenticios foodstuffs

productos de belleza beauty products

productos para ... ... products

programa infantil children's programme/program

prohibida la entrada no entry

prohibida la entrada a menores de ... años no person under ... years of age allowed

prohibida su reproducción copyright reserved

prohibida su venta not for sale

prohibido ... no ...

prohibido adelantar no overtaking, no passing

prohibido aparcar no parking

prohibido aparcar excepto carga y descarga no parking except for loading and unloading

prohibido asomarse a la ventilla do not lean out

prohibido bañarse no swimming

prohibido cambiar de sentido no U-turns

prohibido cantar no singing

prohibido el paso no entry

prohibido escupir no spitting

prohibido estacionar no parking

prohibido fijar carteles stick no bills

prohibido girar a la izquierda no left turn

prohibido hablar con el conductor do not speak to the driver

prohibido hacer auto-stop no hitch-hiking

prohibido hacer sonar el claxon/la bocina do not sound your horn

prohibido pisar el césped keep off the grass

prohibido pisar la hierba keep off the grass

prohibido tirar basura no litter

prohibido tirar escombros no dumping

prohibido tocar la bocina do not sound your horn

prohibido tomar fotografías no photographs

propiedad privada private property

pts (pesetas) pesetas

puchero canario *[poochairo kanar-yo]* casserole containing meat, chickpeas and corn

puente aéreo shuttle (*aircraft*)

puente de fuerte pendiente hump-backed bridge

puente de peaje toll bridge

puente romano Roman bridge

puerta no. gate no.

puerto port

puerto deportivo marina

puesto de socorro first aid post

pulpitos con cebolla *[poolpeetos kon thebo-ya]* baby octopuses with onions

pulpo *[poolpo]* octopus

pulse botón para cruzar press button to cross

pulseras bracelets

¡puñeta! *[poon-yayta]* hell!

puré de patatas *[pooray]* potato puree

puros cigars

purrusalda *[poorroosalda]* cod with leeks and potatoes

Q

¿qué desea? *[kay day-saya]* what can I do for you?

queso con membrillo *[kayso kon mem-bree-yo]* cheese with quince jelly

queso de bola *[kayso]* Dutch cheese

queso de oveja *[kayso day obay-на]* sheep's cheese

queso del país *[kayso del pa-ees]* local cheese

queso gallego *[kayso ga-yaygo]* creamy cheese

queso manchego *[kayso]* hard, strong cheese

¿qué tal? *[kay]* how are you?

quinto piso (*UK*) fifth floor, (*USA*) sixth floor

quiosco kiosk

quisquillas *[keeskee-yas]* shrimps

R

R.A.C.E. (Real Automóvil Club de España) Spanish Royal Automobile Club
rábanos radishes
ración de ... [rath-yon] portion of ...
ragout de ternera [ragoot day tairnaira] veal ragout
rape a la americana [rapay] white fish with brandy and herbs
rape a la cazuela [rapay a la kathwayla] stewed white fish
rape a la plancha [rapay] grilled white fish
raviolis [rab-yolees] ravioli
raya [ra-ya] skate
razón enquire here
rebajas reductions
recepción reception
recibo receipt
recién pintado wet paint
reclamación de equipajes baggage claim
reclamaciones complaints
redondo al horno [orno] roast fillet
reduzca la velocidad reduce speed now
reembolsos refunds
reestreno re-release (of a classic movie)
refrescos cold drinks
regalos gifts
registro de equipajes check-in
registros sanitarios government health certificate
rejoneador bullfighter on horseback
relojería watches and clocks
relojes watches
remolacha beetroot
renacimiento Renaissance
RENFE (Red Nacional de Ferrocarriles españoles) Spanish Railways/Railroad
reparación de calzado shoe repairs
repostería de la casa cakes and desserts made on the premises

repuestos spares
requesón [rekeson] cream cheese/cottage cheese
reserva especial quality wine matured in casks
reservado reserved
reservado el derecho de admisión the management reserve the right to refuse admission
reservado socios members only
reservas reservations
restaurante restaurant
retales remnants
retraso delay
retrete toilets, rest rooms
revuelto de ajos tiernos [rebwelto day aнos t-yairnos] scrambled eggs with spring garlic
revuelto de angulas [rebwelto day angoolas] scrambled eggs with baby eels
revuelto de gambas [rebwelto day gambas] scrambled eggs with prawns
revuelto de sesos [rebwelto] scrambled eggs with brains
revuelto de espárragos trigueros [rebwelto day ... treegairos] scrambled eggs with asparagus
revuelto mixto [rebwelto meesto] scrambled eggs with mixed vegetables
Ribeiro vine growing region in Galicia producing slightly sparkling red and white wines
riñones [reen-yonays] kidneys
riñones al jerez [reen-yonays al Haireth] kidneys with sherry
río ... river ...
Rioja vine growing region in the north producing some of the finest wines in Spain, both reds and whites
rodaballo [rodaba-yo] turbot
románico romanesque
romero [romairo] rosemary
romesco de pescado mixed fish

ron rum
ropa confeccionada ready to wear clothes
ropa de caballeros men's clothes
ropa de cama bed linen
ropa de señoras ladies' clothes

ropa infantil children's clothes
ropa interior underwear
roscas sweet pastries
rovellons [robel-yons] mushrooms (Catalonia)
ruinas ruins

S

S.A. (Sociedad Anónima) PLC, Inc
sábanas sheets
sala climatizada air conditioned cinema/movie theater
sala de banquetes banqueting hall
sala de conciertos concert hall
sala de embarque departure lounge
sala de espera waiting room
sala de exposiciones exhibition hall
sala de tránsito transit lounge
sala especial arts cinema/movie theater
sala X X-rated cinema/movie theater
salchichas sausages
salchichas de Frankfurt frankfurters
salchichón white sausage with pepper
saldo clearance
saldos sales
salida exit
salida ciudad take this direction to leave the city
salida de ambulancias ambulance exit
salida de autopista end of motorway/highway
salida de camiones heavy goods vehicle exit
salida de emergencias emergency exit
salida de fábrica factory exit
salida de incendios fire exit
salidas departures
salidas internacionales international departures
salidas nacionales domestic departures
salmón a la parrilla [sal-mon a la parree-ya] grilled salmon
salmón ahumado [sal-mon a-oomado] smoked salmon
salmón frío [sal-mon] cold salmon

salmonetes [sal-monaytays] red mullet
salmonetes a la parrilla [sal-monaytays a la parree-ya] grilled red mullet
salmonetes en papillote [sal-monaytays em papee-yotay] red mullet cooked in foil
salmorejo [salmoray-ho] marinated fish
salón de belleza beauty salon
salón de demostraciones exhibition hall
salpicón de mariscos shellfish with vinaigrette
salsa allioli/ali oli oil with garlic
salsa bechamel bechamel sauce (white sauce made from cream, butter and flour)
salsa de tomate [tomatay] tomato sauce
salsa holandesa [olandaysa] hot sauce made with eggs and butter
salsa mahonesa/mayonesa [ma-onaysa] mayonnaise
salsa romesco sauce made with peppers, tomato and garlic
salsa tártara tartare sauce
salsa vinagreta sauce vinaigrette
sangría mixture of red wine, lemonade, spirits and fruit
sardinas a la brasa barbecued sardines
sardinas a la parrilla [parree-ya] grilled sardines
sardinas fritas fried sardines
se aceptan tarjetas de crédito we accept credit cards
se alquila for hire, to rent
se alquila habitación room to let/rent
secadores dryers
sección de ... ... department
seco dry

seda natural pure silk
segunda clase second class
segundo piso (*UK*) second floor, (*USA*) third floor
se habla inglés English spoken
sellos stamps
semanarios weeklies
semidulce medium sweet
se necesita ... ... needed
señoras ladies' toilet, ladies' rest room
señores gents' toilet, men's rest room
se precisa ... ... needed
se prohibe fumar no smoking
se prohibe hablar con el conductor do not speak to the driver
se prohibe hacer fuego it is forbidden to light fires
se prohibe la entrada no entry
se prohibe tirar basura no litter
séptimo piso (*UK*) seventh floor, (*USA*) eighth floor
se ruega please
servicio de fotocopias photocopying service
servicio de habitaciones room service
servicio incluido service included
servicios toilets, rest rooms
sesión continua continuous showing
sesión de noche late showing
sesión de tarde early showing
sesión numerada advance booking
sesos a la romana [*saysos*] fried brains in batter
sesos rebozados [*saysos rebothados*] brains in batter
setas a la bordalesa mushrooms
setas a la plancha grilled mushrooms
setas rellenas [*ray-yaynas*] stuffed mushrooms
sexto piso (*UK*) sixth floor, (*USA*) seventh floor
se vende for sale
shangurro (centollo relleno) [*thento-yo ray-yayno*] spider crab cooked in its shell
sí yes
sidra cider
siga adelante straight ahead
siglo de oro XVI-XVII century
silencio silence
sírvase coger una cesta please take a basket
sírvase frío serve cold

sobrecarga excess weight; extra charge
socios associates, members
sólo ... ... only
sólo carga y descarga loading and unloading only
sólo máquinas de afeitar shavers only
solomillo con guisantes [*solomee-yo kon g-eesantays*] fillet steak with peas
solomillo con patatas [*solomee-yo*] fillet steak with potatoes
solomillo de ternera [*solomee-yo day tairnaira*] fillet of veal
solomillo de vaca [*solomee-yo day baca*] fillet of beef
solomillo frío [*solomee-yo*] cold roast beef
sólo motos motorcycles only
solución ... gotas solution ... drops
sombreros hats
somnífero sleeping pill
sopa soup
sopa castellana [*kastay-yana*] vegetable soup
sopa de ajo [*aно*] garlic soup
sopa de almendras almond-based pudding
sopa de cola de buey [*bway*] oxtail soup
sopa de fideos noodle soup
sopa de gallina [*ga-yeena*] chicken soup
sopa de legumbres [*legoombrays*] vegetable soup
sopa de lentejas [*lentay-Has*] lentil soup
sopa de marisco fish and shellfish soup
sopa de pescado fish soup
sopa de rabo de buey [*bway*] oxtail soup
sopa de tortuga [*tortooga*] turtle soup
sopa de verduras [*bairdooras*] vegetable soup
sopa del día soup of the day
sopa mallorquina [*ma-yorkeena*] soup with tomato, meat and eggs
sorbete [*sorbaytay*] sorbet
sótano basement
souffle de fresones strawberry soufflé
souffle de naranja [*naran-нa*] orange soufflé
souffle de queso [*kayso*] cheese soufflé
sr. (señor) Mr.
sra. (señora) Mrs.
sres. (señores) Messrs.
srta. (señorita) Miss
sucursal branch

sugerencias de presentación serving suggestions
super four-star petrol, premium (gas)
supermercado supermarket

suplemento de verduras *[sooplemento day bairdooras]* extra vegetables
sur south
surtido assortment

T

T.V.E. (Television Española) Spanish Television
Tabacalera SA Spanish tobacco monopoly
tabaco tobacco
tablón de anuncios notice board, bulletin board
TALGO luxury train
talla ... size ...
tallarines *[ta-yareenays]* tagliatelle
tallas grandes large sizes
tallas sueltas odd sizes
talón de equipajes baggage slip
taquilla ticket office
tarifas de servicio fares
tarjeta de crédito credit card
tarjeta de embarque boarding card
tarjetas cards
Tarragona vine growing region on the Mediterranean coast producing red and white wines
tarta de almendra almond tart
tarta de chocolate *[chocolatay]* chocolate tart
tarta de fresas strawberry tart
tarta de la casa tart baked on the premises
tarta de manzana *[manthana]* apple tart
tarta helada *[elada]* ice-cream gateau
tarta moca mocha tart (*like coffee, with sponge fingers and almonds*)
tazas cups
teatro theatre, theater
tejidos materials (*cloths*)
teléfono telephone
teléfonos para casos urgentes emergency telephone numbers
telegramas telegrams
televisores television sets
tencas tench (*fish*)

TER express train
tercer piso (*UK*) third floor, (*USA*) fourth floor
terminal internacional international terminal
terminal nacional domestic terminal
ternera asada *[tairnaira]* roast veal
tfno. (teléfono) telephone
tienda de deportes sports shop/store
tienda de discos record shop/store
tienda de electrodomésticos electrical goods shop/store
tienda de lanas woollen goods shop/store
tienda de muebles furniture shop/store
tienda de regalos gift shop/store
Tierra Alta vine growing region in the province of Tarragona producing red and white wines
timbre de alarma alarm bell
tintorería dry cleaner
tirar pull
tiritas elastoplast (*tm*), bandaid
toallas towels
tocadiscos record players
tocinillos de cielo *[totheenee-yos del thyaylo]* crème caramel
tomates rellenos *[tomatays ray-yaynos]* stuffed tomatoes
tómese ... veces al día to be taken ... times per day
tómese antes de las comidas to be taken before meals
tómese después de las comidas to be taken after meals
tónica tonic
tordo thrush
torero bullfighter
tortilla a la paisana *[tortee-ya a la pa-eesana]* omelet(te) containing different

vegetables

tortilla Alaska *[tortee-ya]* baked Alaska

tortilla al ron *[tortee-ya]* omelet(te) with rum

tortilla a su gusto *[tortee-ya a soo goosto]* omelet(te) made as the customer wishes

tortilla de bonito *[tortee-ya]* tuna fish omelet(te)

tortilla de champiñones *[tortee-ya day champeen-yonays]* mushroom omelet(te)

tortilla de chorizo *[tortee-ya day choreetho]* omelet(te) containing spiced sausage

tortilla de escabeche *[tortee-ya day eskabechay]* fish omelet(e)

tortilla de espárragos *[tortee-ya]* asparagus omelet(te)

tortilla de gambas *[tortee-ya]* prawn omelet(te)

tortilla de jamón *[tortee-ya day жamon]* ham omelet(te)

tortilla de patatas *[tortee-ya]* potato omelet(te)

tortilla de sesos *[tortee-ya]* brain omelet(te)

tortilla de setas *[tortee-ya]* mushroom omelet(te)

tortilla española *[tortee-ya espan-yola]* potato omelet(te)

tortillas variadas *[tortee-yas bar-yadas]* various omelet(te)s

tostón asado roast sucking pig

tournedo tournedos (fillet steak)

tóxico poisonous

transferencia transfer

tren de carga goods train

trucha ahumada *[troocha a-oomada]* smoked trout

trucha con jamón *[troocha kon жamon]* trout with ham

trucha escabechada *[troocha]* marinated trout

túnel tunnel

turbante de arroz *[toorbantay day arrooth]* rice served with steak, sausage, peppers and bacon

turrón de coco *[toorron]* coconut nougat

U

Ud (usted) you (*singular*)

Uds (ustedes) you (*plural*)

últimos días last days

ultramarinos grocer

uniformes uniforms

urbanización housing estate

uso externo not to be taken internally

uso obligatorio cinturón de seguridad seatbelts must be worn

Utiel-Requena vine growing region in Valencia producing mild red and rosé wines

V Y Z

vado permanente no parking at any time
vagón restaurante restaurant car
vajillas crockery
Valdeorras vine growing region in Galicia producing red and white wines
Valdepeñas vine growing region of the interior producing pale and dark fruity red wines
Valencia vine growing region on the Mediterranean producing red and white wines
Valle de Monterrey vine growing region in Galicia producing full-bodied red and white wines
valores securities
Vascongadas the Basque Country
vasos glasses (*for drinking*)
Vd (usted) you (*singular*)
Vds (ustedes) you (*plural*)
vehículos pesados heavy vehicles
velocidad controlada speed checks are in operation
velocidad limitada speed limits apply

veneno poison
venta de localidades tickets
venta de sellos we sell stamps
ventas a crédito credit terms available
ventas a plazos hire purchase, installment plan
ventas al contado cash sales
veterinario veterinary surgeon
vía oral orally
vía rectal per rectum
vieiras *[b-yayras]* scallops
vino blanco *[beeno]* white wine
vino de la casa *[beeno]* house wine
vino de jerez *[beeno day Haireth]* sherry
vino de mesa *[beeno]* table wine
vino rosado *[beeno]* rosé wine
vino tinto *[beeno]* red wine
vinos y licores *[beeno ee leekorays]* wines and spirits
vista turística scenic view
voltaje voltage
vo subtitulada with subtitles
vuelo flight

Yecla vine growing region in the south producing smooth red and light rosé wines

zanahorias a la crema *[thana-or-yas]* carrots à la crème
zapatería shoeshop, shoe store
zapatillas slippers
zapatos shoes
zarzuela de mariscos *[tharthwayla]* seafood stew
zarzuela de pescados y mariscos *[tharthwayla]* fish and shellfish stew
zona azul restricted parking area, permit holders only
zona de avalanchas frequent avalanches
zona industrial industrial area
zona monumental historic monuments

zona reservada para peatones pedestrian precinct
zumo de albaricoque *[thoomo day albareekokay]* apricot juice
zumo de lima *[thoomo]* lime juice
zumo de limón *[thoomo]* lemon juice
zumo de melocotón *[thoomo]* peach juice
zumo de naranja *[thoomo day naran-Ha]* orange juice
zumo de piña *[thoomo day peen-ya]* pineapple juice
zumo de tomate *[thoomo day tomatay]* tomato juice

Reference Grammar

NOUNS

GENDER

All nouns in Spanish are either masculine or feminine in gender. Almost all nouns ending in **-o** are masculine and those ending in **-a**, **-ión** or **-ad** are feminine. Nouns with other endings may be either gender.

PLURALS

To form the plurals of nouns, follow the rules given below:

ending of noun

any vowel	add **-s**
any consonant	add **-es**
-z	change **-z** to **-ces**

For example:

el vino	**los vinos**	the wine(s)
el hotel	**los hoteles**	the hotel(s)
la luz	**las luces**	the light(s)

ARTICLES

THE DEFINITE ARTICLE (THE)
The form of the definite article depends on whether the noun is masculine or feminine, singular or plural:

	sing.	pl.
m.	**el**	**los**
f.	**la**	**las**

For example:

el restaurante	**los restaurantes**	the restaurant(s)
la playa	**las playas**	the beach(es)

Note that **a** + **el** (to the) becomes **al**, and **de** + **el** (of the) becomes **del**:

al lado del café   next to the cafe
detrás del coche   behind the car

THE INDEFINITE ARTICLE (A, AN, SOME)
This also varies according to whether the noun is masculine or feminine, singular or plural:

	sing.	pl.
m.	**un**	**unos**
f.	**una**	**unas**

For example:

un coche	**unos coches**	a car (cars *or* some cars)
una oficina	**unas oficinas**	an office (offices *or* some offices)

ADJECTIVES

Adjectives in Spanish usually follow the noun they refer to and change their form according to whether the noun is masculine or feminine, singular or plural.

To find the feminine form:

change the masculine ending	to
-o	-a
-or	-ora
-és	-esa
-ón	-ona

In most other cases the masculine and feminine forms are the same.
The plurals of adjectives are formed according to the rules which apply to nouns.
For example:

los vasos grandes   the big glasses
las botellas pequeñas   the small bottles

COMPARATIVES (BIGGER, BETTER etc)

Comparatives are formed by placing **más** in front of the adjective:
bonito   nice   **más bonito**   nicer

To say that something is 'more ... than ...' use **más ... que ...**:
soy más alta que mi hermana   I am taller than my sister

To say that something is 'as ... as ...' use **tan ... como ...**:
es tan alto como su amigo   he is as tall as your friend

SUPERLATIVES (BIGGEST, BEST etc)

The superlative is formed by placing **el** or **la más** in front of the adjective:

bonito nice   **más bonito** nicer   **el más bonito** *or* **la más bonita** nicest

Note that 'in' following a superlative in English is expressed by **de** in Spanish:

es la habitación más grande del hotel   it's the biggest room
                                             in the hotel

A few adjectives have irregular comparatives and superlatives:

bueno	good	**mejor**	better	**el mejor**	the best
grande	big	**mayor**	bigger/older	**el mayor**	the biggest/oldest
malo	bad	**peor**	worse	**el peor**	the worst
pequeño	small	**menor**	younger	**el menor**	the youngest

POSSESSIVE ADJECTIVES (MY, YOUR etc)

As with other adjectives, their form depends on the gender and number of the noun they refer to. The possessive adjectives are:

	m. sing.	f. sing.	m. pl.	f. pl.
my	mi	mi	mis	mis
your (sing. familiar)	tu	tu	tus	tus
his/her/its; your (sing. formal)	su	su	sus	sus
our	nuestro	nuestra	nuestros	nuestras
your (pl. familiar)	vuestro	vuestra	vuestros	vuestras
their; your (pl. formal)	su	su	sus	sus

For example:

tus maletas	your suitcases
nuestro apartamento	our apartment
mi hotel	my hotel

Since **su** can mean 'his', 'her', 'its', 'your' or 'their' the following may be used instead, placed after the noun, to avoid confusion:

de él	his
de ella	her
de Usted	your (sing. formal)
de ellos	their (m.)
de ellas	their (f.)
de Ustedes	your (pl. formal)

For example:

la habitación de ella	her room
el amigo de Usted	your friend
el pasaporte de él	his passport

DEMONSTRATIVE ADJECTIVES (THIS, THAT etc)

Demonstrative adjectives are placed before the noun, and their form also depends on the gender and number of the noun. There are three demonstrative adjectives in Spanish:

este	this (referring to an object near the speaker)
ese	that (referring to an object near the person the speaker is addressing)
aquel	that (referring to an object distant from both the speaker and the person addressed)

The forms of the demonstrative adjectives are:

	este	ese	aquel
m. sing.	**este**	**ese**	**aquel**
f. sing.	**esta**	**esa**	**aquella**
m. pl.	**estos**	**esos**	**aquellos**
f. pl.	**estas**	**esas**	**aquellas**

For example:

este hotel	this hotel
esas niñas	those girls
aquellas mujeres	those women

PRONOUNS

PERSONAL PRONOUNS

subject		direct object		indirect object	
yo	I	**me**	me	**me**	to me
tú	you (sing. familiar)	**te**	you	**te**	to you
él	he	**le**	him	**le**	to him
ella	she	**la**	her	**le**	to her
Usted	you (sing. formal)	**le/la**	you	**le**	to you
		lo/la	it		
nosotros/as	we (m./f.)	**nos**	us	**nos**	to us
vosotros/as	you (pl. familiar) (m./f.)	**os**	you	**os**	to you
ellos	they (m.)	**les**	them	**les**	to them
ellas	they (f.)	**las**	them	**les**	to them
Ustedes	you (pl. formal)	**les/las**	you	**les**	to you

Pronouns expressing the subject are often omitted in Spanish as the ending of the verb makes it clear who is carrying out an action. For example, **hablo** can only mean 'I speak'. But when different subjects take the same ending of the verb, e.g. with the he/she/it/you forms, subject pronouns may be used to avoid confusion. They are also used to place emphasis on the subject.

For example:

| **yo quiero un café** | *I* want a cup of coffee |
| **él no quiere ir** | *he* doesn't want to go |

Personal pronouns in Spanish usually come before the verb:

| **me molesta** | he's annoying me |

However, when they are used with a command, an infinitive or the form of the verb ending in **-ando** or **-iendo** (meaning '-ing'), they are tacked on to the end of the verb and form a single word with it:

díga*me*	tell me
quiero cambiar*la*	I want to change it
está comprándo*lo*	she is buying it

YOU

There are two ways of expressing 'you' in Spanish. They are:

tú (sing.) and **vosotros** (pl.)	used to address friends, relatives and children and also used between young people. Verb endings with these are **-as** or **-es** in the singular and **-áis**, **-éis** or **-ís** in the plural.
Usted (sing.) and **Ustedes** (pl.)	more formal, used to address people the speaker doesn't know well. Verb endings with these are **-a** or **-e** in the singular and **-an** or **-en** in the plural.

For example:

¿queréis algo de beber?	would you like a drink?
¿qué desea Usted?	what would you like?

REFLEXIVE PRONOUNS (MYSELF, YOURSELF etc)

Reflexive verbs are those with which the object is the same as the subject, e.g. I wash (myself). The reflexive pronouns are:

me	myself
te	yourself (sing. familiar)
se	himself/herself/itself; yourself (sing. formal)
nos	ourselves
os	yourselves (pl. familiar)
se	themselves; yourselves (pl. formal)

Spanish uses many more verbs reflexively than English.

For example:

me levanto a las siete	I get up at seven
los niños se acuestan a las ocho	the children go to bed at eight
nos paseamos por la ciudad	we stroll around the city

POSSESSIVE PRONOUNS (MINE, YOURS etc)

The possessive pronouns are:

	m. sing.	f. sing.	m. pl.	f. pl.
mine	**el mío**	**la mía**	**los míos**	**las mías**
yours (sing. familiar)	**el tuyo**	**la tuya**	**los tuyos**	**las tuyas**
his/hers; yours (sing. formal)	**el suyo**	**la suya**	**los suyos**	**las suyas**
ours	**el nuestro**	**la nuestra**	**los nuestros**	**las nuestras**
yours (pl. familiar)	**el vuestro**	**la vuestra**	**los vuestros**	**las vuestras**
theirs; yours (pl. formal)	**el suyo**	**la suya**	**los suyos**	**las suyas**

Like the possessive adjectives, possessive pronouns agree in number and gender with the object possessed:

no es mi pasaporte, es el suyo   it isn't my passport, it's yours
son las suyas   they are yours

DEMONSTRATIVE PRONOUNS (THIS ONE, THAT ONE etc)

These are identical to the demonstrative adjectives (see page 104), but are written with an accent:

éste   **ése**   **aquél**

Neuter forms also exist which are used when no specific noun is being referred to:

¿qué es esto?   what is this?
eso es absurdo   that's absurd

VERBS

Spanish verbs are divided into three groups:

those ending in **-ar**	e.g. **hablar**–to speak
those ending in **-er**	e.g. **comer**–to eat
those ending in **-ir**	e.g. **vivir**–to live

THE PRESENT TENSE

To form the present tense, take off the **-ar**, **-er** or **ir** endings and add the present tense endings:

hablar		**comer**		**vivir**	
habl-o	I speak	**com-o**	I eat	**viv-o**	I live
habl-as	you speak (sing. (familiar)	**com-es**	you eat (sing. (familiar)	**viv-es**	you live (sing. (familiar)
habl-a	he/she/it speaks; you speak (sing. formal)	**com-e**	he/she/it eats; you eat (sing. formal)	**viv-e**	he/she/it lives; you live (sing. formal)
habl-amos	we speak	**com-emos**	we eat	**viv-imos**	we live
habl-áis	you speak (pl. familiar)	**com-éis**	you eat (pl. familiar)	**viv-ís**	you live (pl. familiar)
habl-an	they speak; you speak (pl. formal)	**com-en**	they eat; you eat (pl. formal)	**viv-en**	they live; you live (pl. formal)

Most verbs are regular and follow the above pattern, but a number change the main vowel in the 'I', 'you', 'he' and 'they' forms. There are three possible changes:

> **o → ue**
> **e → ie**
> **e → i**

For example:
costar	— **¿cuánto cuesta?**	how much does it cost?
sentir	— **no me siento bien**	I don't feel well
decir	— **¿qué dices?**	what are you saying?

Some common verbs have irregular present tenses:

tener (to have)	**dar** (to give)	**ir** (to go)	**venir** (to come)
tengo	**doy**	**voy**	**vengo**
tienes	**das**	**vas**	**vienes**
tiene	**da**	**va**	**viene**
tenemos	**damos**	**vamos**	**venimos**
tenéis	**dais**	**vais**	**venís**
tienen	**dan**	**van**	**vienen**

The following verbs are irregular in the 'I' form only:

hacer	to do	**hago**
salir	to come/go out	**salgo**
poner	to put	**pongo**
saber	to know	**sé**
decir	to say	**digo**

THE PAST TENSE

Two past tenses are commonly used in Spanish.

The IMPERFECT TENSE is used to express an action which was repeated over a period of time (like the meaning of 'used to' in English) and is formed as follows:

hablar	comer	vivir
habl-aba	com-ía	viv-ía
habl-abas	com-ías	viv-ías
habl-aba	com-ía	viv-ía
habl-ábamos	com-íamos	viv-íamos
habl-abais	com-íais	viv-íais
habl-aban	com-ían	viv-ían

The verb **ser** (to be) has the only irregular imperfect:

era	I was
eras	you were (sing. familiar)
era	he/she/it was;
	you were (sing. formal)
éramos	we were
erais	you were (pl. familiar)
eran	they were;
	you were (pl. formal)

The PERFECT TENSE is used to express a completed action in the past. It is formed by using the verb **haber** (to have) and the past participle of the verb. The forms of **haber** are:

he	I have
has	you have (sing. familiar)
ha	he/she/it has;
	you have (sing. formal)
hemos	we have
habéis	you have (pl. familiar)
han	they have;
	you have (pl. formal)

Past participles are formed by dropping the **-ar** ending and adding **-ado**, or by dropping **-er** or **-ir** and adding **-ido.**

For example:

he hablado	I have spoken
han salido	they have gone out
hemos comido	we have eaten

A few verbs have irregular past participles:

hacer	to make/do	**hecho**
abrir	to open	**abierto**
volver	to go/come back	**vuelto**
ver	to see	**visto**
decir	to say	**dicho**
poner	to put	**puesto**

THE FUTURE TENSE

The future tense is formed by adding the following endings to the **-ar**, **-er** or **ir** forms:

hablar	comer	vivir
hablar-é	**comer-é**	**vivir-é**
hablar-ás	**comer-ás**	**vivir-ás**
hablar-á	**comer-á**	**vivir-á**
hablar-emos	**comer-emos**	**vivir-emos**
hablar-éis	**comer-éis**	**vivir-éis**
hablar-án	**comer-án**	**vivir-án**

A few verbs add these endings to a modified form of the verb:

tener	**tendré**	I will have
hacer	**haré**	I will make/do
decir	**diré**	I will say
venir	**vendré**	I will come
salir	**saldré**	I will come/go out
poner	**pondré**	I will put
poder	**podré**	I will be able

MAKING THE VERB NEGATIVE

By putting **no** in front of the verb, it is made negative:

no tengo calor	I am not hot
no quiero ir a una discoteca	I don't want to go to a disco

no is also used in conjunction with other negatives:

no... nada	nothing, not... anything
no... nunca	never
no... nadie	nobody, not... anybody
	no one, not... anyone
no... ninguno	none, not... any

For example:

no quiero nada más	I don't want anything else
no fumo nunca	I never smoke
no hay nadie en el comedor	there is nobody in the dining-room
no tengo ninguno	I don't have any

THE IMPERATIVE (GIVING COMMANDS)

The forms used for people addressed as **tú** and **vosotros** are:

sing.:	**habl-a**	**com-e**	**abr-e**
pl.:	**habl-ad**	**com-ed**	**abr-id**

For people addressed as **Usted** and **Ustedes** the forms are:

sing.:	**habl-e**	**com-a**	**abr-a**
pl.:	**habl-en**	**com-an**	**abr-an**

Verbs which are irregular in the 'I' form have the same irregularity in the imperative (see page 109):

haga esto	do this
ponga el sombrero en la mesa	put the hat on the table

To make the imperative negative, **no** is placed in front of the verb. In the case of the **tú** and **vosotros** forms, the verb endings also change:

a → es	**ad → éis**
e→as	**ed → áis**
	id → áis

For example:

no bebáis eso	don't drink that
no mires	don't look
no cierres el coche	don't lock the car

Pronouns are placed after the imperative:

cómpralo	buy it
ábrelos	open them

but when the imperative is negative they are placed in front of it:

no lo compres	don't buy it
no los abras	don't open them

TO BE

There are two verbs meaning to 'be' in Spanish – **ser** and **estar**.

The present tense forms of these are:

ser		estar
soy	I am	**estoy**
eres	you are (sing. familiar)	**estás**
es	he/she/it is; you are (sing. formal)	**está**
somos	we are	**estamos**
sois	you are (pl. familiar)	**estáis**
son	they are; you are (pl. formal)	**están**

Ser is used to express permanent qualities. It is used with nationalities and occupations as well as with expressions of time and in impersonal expressions:

For example:

mi bolso es blanco	my bag is white
soy inglés	I am English
¿es Usted médico?	are you a doctor?
son las dos	it's two o'clock
es fácil	it's easy

Estar is used to express position and temporary states:

For example:

Pedro está cansado	Peter is tired
el hotel está cerca de la playa	the hotel is near the beach

TELLING THE TIME

what time is it?	¿qué hora es? *[kay **o**ra es]*
it is ...	es ...(for one o'clock)
	son las ... (after one o'clock)
one o'clock	la una *[**oo**na]*
seven o'clock	las siete *[s-**yay**tay]*
one a.m.	la una de la mañana *[**oo**na day la man-**ya**na]*
seven a.m.	las siete de la mañana *[s-**yay**tay day la man-**ya**na]*
one p.m.	la una de la tarde *[**oo**na day la **ta**rday]*
seven p.m.	las siete de la tarde *[s-**yay**tay day la **ta**rday]*
midday	mediodía *[maid-yo**dee**-a]*
midnight	medianoche *[maid-yan**o**chay]*
five past eight	las ocho y cinco *[ee th**ee**nko]*
five to eight	las ocho menos cinco *[**th**eenko]*
half past ten	las diez y media *[d-yayth ee **ma**id-ya]*
quarter past eleven	las once y cuarto *[**o**nthay ee **kwa**rto]*
quarter to eleven	las once menos un cuarto *[**ma**ynos oon **kwa**rto]*

CONVERSION TABLES

1. LENGTH

centimetres, centimeters
1 cm = 0.39 inches

metres, meters
1 m = 100 cm = 1000 mm
1 m = 39.37 inches = 1.09 yards

kilometres, kilometers
1 km = 1000 m
1 km = 0.62 miles = 5/8 mile

km	1	2	3	4	5	10	20	30	40	50	100
miles	0.6	1.2	1.9	2.5	3.1	6.2	12.4	18.6	24.9	31.1	62.1

inches
1 inch = 2.54 cm

feet
1 foot = 30.48 cm

yards
1 yard = 0.91 m

miles
1 mile = 1.61 km = 8/5 km

miles	1	2	3	4	5	10	20	30	40	50	100
km	1.6	3.2	4.8	6.4	8.0	16.1	32.2	48.3	64.4	80.5	161

2. WEIGHT

gram(me)s
1 g = 0.035 oz

g	100	250	500
oz	3.5	8.75	17.5 = 1.1 lb

kilos

1 kg = 1000 g
1 kg = 2.20 lb = 11/5 lb

kg	0.5	1	1.5	2	3	4	5	6	7	8	9	10
lb	1.1	2.2	3.3	4.4	6.6	8.8	11.0	13.2	15.4	17.6	19.8	22

kg	20	30	40	50	60	70	80	90	100
lb	44	66	88	110	132	154	176	198	220

tons

1 UK ton = 1018 kg
1 US ton = 909 kg

tonnes

1 tonne = 1000 kg
1 tonne = 0.98 UK tons = 1.10 US tons

ounces

1 oz = 28.35 g

pounds

1 pound = 0.45 kg = 5/11 kg

lb	1	1.5	2	3	4	5	6	7	8	9	10	20
kg	0.5	0.7	0.9	1.4	1.8	2.3	2.7	3.2	3.6	4.1	4.5	

stones

1 stone = 6.35 kg

stones	1	2	3	7	8	9	10	11	12	13	14	15
kg	6.3	12.7	19	44	51	57	63	70	76	83	89	95

hundredweights

1 UK hundredweight = 50.8 kg
1 US hundredweight = 45.36 kg

3. CAPACITY

litres, liters

1 l = 7.6 UK pints = 2.13 US pints
½ l = 500 cl
¼ l = 250 cl

pints
1 UK pint = 0.57 l
1 US pint = 0.47 l

quarts
1 UK quart = 1.14 l
1 US quart = 0.95 l

gallons
1 UK gallon = 4.55 l
1 US gallon = 3.79 l

4. TEMPERATURE

centigrade/Celsius
$C = (F - 32) \times 5/9$

C	−5	0	5	10	15	18	20	25	30	37	38
F	23	32	41	50	59	64	68	77	86	98.4	100.4

Fahrenheit
$F = (C \times 9/5) + 32$

F	23	32	40	50	60	65	70	80	85	98.4	101
C	−5	0	4	10	16	20	21	27	30	37	38.3

NUMBERS

0	cero *[thairo]*		
1	uno *[oono]*	1st	primero *[preemairo]*
2	dos	2nd	segundo *[segoondo]*
3	tres	3rd	tercero *[tairthairo]*
4	cuatro *[kwatro]*	4th	cuarto *[kwarto]*
5	cinco *[theenko]*	5th	quinto *[keento]*
6	seis *[says]*	6th	sexto *[sesto]*
7	siete *[s-yaytay]*	7th	séptimo
8	ocho	8th	octavo *[oktabo]*
9	nueve *[nway-bay]*	9th	nono
10	diez *[d-yayth]*	10th	décimo *[detheemo]*
11	once *[onthay]*		
12	doce *[dothay]*		
13	trece *[trethay]*		
14	catorce *[katorthay]*		
15	quince *[keenthay]*		
16	dieciséis *[d-yaythee—]*		
17	diecisiete *[d-yaythee—]*		
18	dieciocho *[d-yaythee—]*		
19	diecinueve *[d-yaythee—]*		
20	veinte *[bayntay]*		
21	veintiuno *[bayntee—]*		
22	veintidós *[bayntee—]*		
23	veintitrés *[bayntee—]*		
etc			
30	treinta *[traynta]*		
31	treinta y uno		
40	cuaranta *[kwarenta]*		
50	cincuenta *[theenkwenta]*		
60	sesenta		
70	setenta		
80	ochenta		
90	noventa *[nobenta]*		
100	cien *[th-yen]*		
101	ciento uno *[th-yento]*		
200	doscientos *[dosth-yentos]*		
300	trescientos		
400	cuatrocientos		
500	quinientos *[keen-yentos]*		
600	seiscientos		
700	setecientos		
800	ochocientos		
900	novecientos *[nobay—]*		
1000	mil *[meel]*		
1987	mil novecientos ochenta y siete *[meel nobayth-yentos ochenta ee s-yaytay]*		
2000	dos mil		